PYTHON PROGRAMMING

This Book Includes:

Learning Python and Python Machine Learning. A Complete Overview for Beginners. How to Master Python Coding Basics and Effectively Learn Faster Computer Programming

Samuel Hack

Copyright © 2019 by Samuel Hack - All rights reserved

The book is only for personal use. No part of this publication may be reproduced, distributed, or transmitted in any form or by any means, including photocopying, recording, or other electronic or mechanical methods, without the prior written permission of the publisher, except in the case of brief quotations embodied in critical reviews and certain other noncommercial uses permitted by copyright law.

TABLE OF CONTENTS

LEARNING PYTHON:

PYTHON MACHINE LEARNING:

LEARNING PYTHON

The Ultimate Guide to Learning How to Develop Applications for Beginners with Python Programming Language Using Numpy, Matplotlib, Scipy and Scikit-learn

INTRODUCTION

Congratulations on purchasing *Learning Python,* and thank you for doing so.

The following chapters will discuss all of the different options and things that you need to know when it comes to working with the Python coding language. There may be a ton of other coding languages out there, all with their proponents and those who will only ever use this kind of coding language for their needs. But for many coders, whether they are just learning how to code for the first time or they are more advanced and have been doing their coding for a very long time, Python is one of the best options to work with.

This guidebook is going to delve a bit into the basics of working with the Python language and will explore more about what Python is all about. We will start out this guidebook with a good introduction to what Python is, some of the benefits of working with this language, and even some of the basic parts that come with a Python code so that anyone, even a beginner, will be ready to take it to the next level when we work on some of the examples of writing code later.

From there, we are going to explore what it means when we say that Python is an OOP language, and how the classes and objects work in this language. We will also look at some of the other neat things that you are able to do within the Python language including how to write loops, working with the decision control statements, how to raise an exception, and even how to work with inheritances and regular expressions.

The end of this guidebook is going to move on from some of the basics of writing codes in Python and will delve a bit deeper into what you are able to do with some of the Python libraries. We will focus mainly on what is possible with the Scikit-Learn library but will explore some of the other options when you are ready to take your coding to the next level.

There are so many benefits that come with working on the Python coding language, and so many people love working with this to help them create any kind of program. When you are ready to learn how to make this coding language work the best for your needs and you want to learn some of the different parts so that you can start writing your own codes, make sure to check out this guidebook to get started.

There are plenty of books on this subject on the market, thanks again for choosing this one! Every effort was made to ensure it is full of as much useful information as possible. Please enjoy!

CHAPTER 1: WHAT IS PYTHON?

There are a lot of different coding languages that you are able to work with. The option that you choose is often going to depend on the amount of experience that you have along with what you are trying to do inside the code that you want to right. Some coding languages are going to be a bit more advanced, some are going to work best with some websites, and some are going to work best with one kind of operating system or another. Each of these coding languages is going to provide you with some benefits, and choosing one as a beginner is going to seem like a big challenge for a beginner.

Even though there are a ton of options that come with coding languages, you will find that one of the best options, whether you are a beginner or more advanced in coding, is Python. You will find that the Python language is simple to use, while still allowing you to really work on some high-quality coding, without posing all of the challenges to a beginner. In fact, this coding language is often one that is recommended to those who are brand new to coding and have never been able to work with any kind of coding in the past.

There are a lot of things to love about this kind of language. It is easy to work with and learn, even with all of the power that comes with it. You will be able to write codes in no time, and the wording is in English, unlike some of the other options you can choose out there, which make it a bit easier to work with overall. And the other tools, like having some good libraries, help from many other people in the coding world, open source programming that is free and more makes it the perfect option when you are first getting started with this kind of language.

You will find that there are a lot of benefits that come with the Python language. The first benefit that we are going to take a look at is the support libraries. You will find that just by opening up the Python language, there are a lot of options available in the library. And you can look at third-party libraries and extensions that can easily be added to this coding language.

This is a great option for you, whether you are a beginner or more advanced with your coding. It is going to provide you with a lot of options on what you are able to do with your coding and can make things easier. You will be able to add in a lot of classes, objects, and functions in this, and that can make life so much easier overall. You can always work just with the libraries and extensions that come with the Python language when you download it, or you can go through and add in some third party libraries to this if you would like some special features and more to work on your codes.

There are a lot of different benefits that are going to help you to really see results with the Python code. You will first enjoy that this is going to be a great option because of all the options that work in the library. The library is going to have a lot of neat codes and options that you are able to work with, that makes it easier for the beginner to get started.

There are also a lot of different options that you can do with this code. It has a ton of power behind it, which many beginners worry that they are not going to be able to learn how to work with this. You will be able to do a ton of things when it comes to this language, whether you have been able to code or not. And it is easily comparable to a lot of the more complicated coding languages that are out there. It may have included a lot of power with it, but it was going to be easy enough to help you to make any code that you want, even if you are a big beginner and have never worked on this kind of coding before.

There is also a large community to use when you are working with Python. There are a lot of programmers, whether they are brand new to coding or have been doing it for some time, which will use this coding language. This allows you to ask questions and find a lot of communities that you are able to work with and see results. This makes it so much easier for you to see how to do things, to get your questions answered, and so much more.

HOW TO INSTALL THE PYTHON LANGUAGE

Now that we know a bit more about using the Python language and why it is going to be a good tool to work with, it is time to move on and figure out what steps you need to follow in order to make sure that the Python language is set up and installed on your computer. You want to make sure that you get the Python code set up on the computer in the proper manner, to ensure that you are able to write out some of the codes that you need, without ending up with any struggles or errors along the way.

Before you, as a programmer will be able to look through some of the other parts of this guidebook and before you are able to work with writing some of your own codes, you need to make sure that the Python language is set up and that you are able to set up the interpreter. Installation for Python is going to be depending on the kind of operating system that is on your computer, along with the installation source that you would like to work with. You do get a few choices when you pick out the source of downloading the Python code, but to make things as easy as possible, we are going to work with www.python.org.

This is why we are going to spend some time looking at the way that you will need to install the Python interpreter and the steps that you can use based on the operating system that you are going to use it on. Let's divide up this chapter and look at some of the different steps that you can use to make this work for you.

HOW TO INSTALL THE MAC OS X

If you plan to use the Python coding language on a Mac operating system when you are ready to install the system, you will find that the Python 2 version should already be on the system, even before you do anything else with it. The exact version of this though is often going to depend on when you got the computer and how old it is. If you are curious about which Python version is on your computer, you just need to open up the prompt for commands and type in the code "python – V." This will list out the version number of Python that is already on the computer so you can decide if that is the one that you want to use or not.

Now, you may decide that you want to use a newer version of Python and even with Python 3. There are a lot of people who would like to change this up, and there are a few steps that you are able to work with, in order to get it all set up into any version of Python that you would like to use. We want to work with Python 3 to make things easier. To check out if the computer has a Python 3 installation on your system, you first need to make sure that you open up the terminal app that we had from before, and type in the code "python3 – V" to see if it is there.

The default with the Mac system, unless you or someone else already installed it on your system, is that Python 3 will not be found on your computer. This means that we need to do the work to get it installed on your computer by visiting the website of www.python.org. This is often the easiest place to start because it is going to include all of the different parts that you need to make the code work. This means that it is going to include all of the tools that are needed the IDLE, the shell, and the interpreter.

Being able to run the IDLE and the shell with this language is going to depend on the specific version of the Python that you want to work with, and you can even choose base on your own preferences when you are doing the coding. The two commands that work the best to make this happen will include:

For Python 2.X just type in "Idle"

For Python 3.X, just type in "idle3"

As we brought up before, when you actually stop and take the time to install and download your Python 3 program on an operating system with Mac, you will need to install the IDLE at the same time to make sure that you are able to do the codes. If you get Python from python.org, you will be fine, and everything will be installed at the same time. If you decide to install this from somewhere else, you will need to check that all of the parts are found there or not, and then install what doesn't seem to show up.

INSTALLING PYTHON ON THE WINDOWS SYSTEM

Now, it is possible for you to download your Python program on a Windows System rather than on a Mac system. You may want to make sure that it is added onto this kind of computer, and you will have to go through a few steps. Windows has its own coding language already found on it, which means that it is not going to have the Python code on it. You will need to go through the right steps in order to get it on the system. It will work just fine on a Windows computer, but you do need to take the steps necessary to get it all installed on your computer.

When you are ready to work with adding the Python language on a computer that has Windows on it, you will need to go through and come up with the right variables for the environment that are needed so that you can bring up the Python commands, just using the prompt. The steps that are needed to help you get the Python code set up on a Windows computer includes:

To set this up, you need to visit the official Python download page and grab the Windows installer. You can choose to do the latest version of Python 3, or go with another option. By default, the installer is going to provide you with the 32-bit version of Python, but you can choose to switch this to the 64-bit version if you wish. The 32-bit is often best to make sure that there aren't any compatibility issues with the older packages, but you can experiment if you wish.

Now right click on the installer and select "Run as Administrator." There are going to be two options to choose from. You will want to pick out "Customize Installation."

On the following screen, make sure all of the boxes under "Optional Features" are clicked and then click to move on.

While under Advanced Options," you should pick out the location where you want Python to be installed. Click on Install. Give it some time to finish and then close the installer.

Next, set the PATH variable for the system so that it includes directories that will include packages and other components that you will need later. To do this, use the following instructions:

Open up the Control Panel. Do this by clicking on the taskbar and typing in Control Panel. Click on the icon.

Inside the Control Panel, search for Environment. Then click on Edit the System Environment Variables. From here, you can click on the button for Environment Variables.

Go to the section for User Variables. You can edit the PATH variable that is there, or you can create one.

If there isn't a variable for PATH on the system, then create one by clicking on New. Make the name for the PATH variable and add in the directories that you want. Click on close all the control Panel dialogs and move on.

Now you can open up your command prompt. Do this by clicking on Start Menu, then Windows System, and then Command Prompt. Type in "python." This is going to load up the Python interpreter for you.

After you have been able to go through some of these steps, don't worry the steps are easier than you would think, you will be able to go through and open up the programming for Python. You can then use this in any manner that you want, just like you would with any other system. You can then take some time to set up the interpreter in the manner that you would like, write out the codes that we have in this guidebook and more, and create any kind of program that you would like.

INSTALLING PYTHON ON A LINUX OPERATING SYSTEM

We can also take some time to install the Python language on a Linux operating system. This is an operating system that a lot of people like to work with because it is simple and allows you to do a lot of things that you may not have been able to do on other programs. It is often seen as one of the easiest operating systems to use when it comes to downloading and working with the Python language, so if you are still on the fence about which operating system to use, then it may be worth your time to work with Linux.

The steps to get the Python coding language on your computer will be a bit different compared to some of the other operating systems that we have talked about before. Some of the codes and the steps that you will need to use in order to get the Python coding language, and all of the things that go with it, installed on your computer include:

$ python3 - - version

If you are on Ubuntu 16.10 or newer, then it is a simple process to install Python 3.6. You just need to use the following commands:

$ sudo apt-get update

$ sudo apt-get installs Python3.6

If you are relying on an older version of Ubuntu or another version, then you may want to work with the deadsnakes PPA, or another tool, to help you download the Python 3.6 version. The code that you need to do this includes:

$ sudo apt-get installs software-properties-common

$ sudo add-apt repository ppa:deadsnakes/ppa

 # suoda apt-get update

$ sudo apt-get installs python3.6

While this does include a bit more code writing than what you are going to see with some of the other operating systems, for the most part, the different distributions of Linux are going to already have Python 3 on them. You can double check to see if this is true. Sometimes the Python 3 may not be on this system for one reason or another, or you will want to go through and update the system a bit to make sure it has what you would like, and you can do that using the codes that we wrote above.

A LOOK AT THE INTERPRETER

Before we dive into some of the different codes that you are able to work with when it comes to Python, we need to understand a bit more about some of the parts that come with the language, and the things that you need to include with it to see the best results. We need to first start with the interpreter for Python. The standard installation that you are able to receive when you download this language from www.python.org is going to have the interpreter, along with all of the other parts that are needed in order to start some of your codings. This means that all of the files, the interpreter, the licensing, the documentation, and more are all going to be found in the download that you need.

The three files that will come with the Python download are going to include the IDLE, the shell, and the interpreter. First, let's take a look at the interpreter for Python. This is something that is important to work with because it is the part of the program that can execute any and all codes that you write. The interpreter is going to take in all of the lines of code that you write and can send them as instructions to be read. It will do the job of processing the orders that you tell it, and executing the code on the screen.

Once you have a good interpreter in place, it is time to work with the Python IDLE. The IDLE is going to stand for integrated development and learning environment. You want to have this in place because it is going to be responsible for holding onto each and every tool that you need when it is time to create some new programs with Python. The right IDLE will hold onto the options for debugging your code, the text editor, and the shell that you will like to use when writing your codes. The IDLE can have a lot of features, or you can keep it basic, and that is going to depend on your own preferences along with which version of Python you would like to use.

If you go to the www.python.org version and decide to download that for your needs, then the IDLE is going to come with that download. However, you may notice that there are a lot of third party options that you can choose if you want to work with a different kind of IDLE in the process. If you are going to be writing a specific type of code for your program or you would like to have some different features with your IDLE, then you can download those at this time and use them as well.

Now, before we end this chapter, we need also to take a look at what is known as the Python Shell. The Shell is like an interactive command line driving interface that is found inside of the interpreter that you use. The Shell is important because it will hold onto all of the commands that you decide to write out, and then it will be the part that actually executes that code that you are working with. Any time that you write out a piece of code that is not understandable or that the compiler is not able to work with, the Shell is going to send you an error message, allowing you to know that something is wrong and that you need to go back through and fix it all up.

It is important to be able to add all of these parts to the Python program before you get started with writing in any of the codes that you want. They may sound a bit complicated, and it may seem like a lot of stuff, but without it, you are going to end up with a mess, and the codes are not going to execute the way that you want.

Keep in mind that you are able to go out and get these from a third party source if you would like, but this is often going to add more work and more confusion to the process. As a beginner, if you simply go to the www.python.org part that we talked about before, select the version of Python that you want to go with along with the operating system that is on your computer, you will be able to download the version and it will contain all of the files and the information that you need to get started. This may limit the features that you get to use a bit, but it will make things easier because you won't have to worry about finding the parts later on before writing the code.

There are a lot of different benefits that come with working on the Python language. Whether you have never coded in the past or you are looking to add another language to your set of skills in coding, Python is going to have exactly what you need. And now that you are this far, all the parts that you need in order to write good strong codes will be in place and ready for you to use.

CHAPTER 2: THE BASICS OF THE PYTHON CODE

Now that we have the Python code set up on our computers and ready to go, it is time to look at some of the different parts that are needed to write out your codes in Python. There are a lot of different types of codes that you are able to write out, but they are going to all come with the same basic parts. Learning these will help you to get more done with your coding, and will ensure that your codes will work with the compiler. Let's take a look at some of the basic parts that come with the Python code, and how you are able to use these to your own advantage to see the best results.

LEARNING THE KEYWORDS

The first part of the Python code that we need to take a look at will be the keywords. There are going to be keywords with any kind of coding language that you are working with, and Python is no different here. These keywords are going to be reserved, and are pretty special because they basically tell your compiler what it needs to do.

These keywords are important because of their one job, which is that they are going to provide the compiler with some commands, and will make sure that the compiler is going to do what you would like. These keywords are going to be important to all of the codes that you decide to do, so make sure that you learn what the keywords are so that you can get the compiler to do what you would like.

WORKING TO NAME YOUR IDENTIFIERS

After you have had some time working with the keywords, it is time to look at the identifiers and how we are able to name them. There are actually several types of identifiers that you are able to work, and they will go by names like classes, entities, functions, and variables. Any time that you want to make sure that you are working with an identifier, you will be able to follow the same rules so once you learn it once, you will be all set with this one and able to name all of the identifiers the same way.

So, we need first to take a look at some of the rules that come with naming the identifiers. First, we have to make sure that we carefully choose the names that you choose because you want to make sure that you can remember them later on. There are many different choices that come with the names you can pick, and you can choose from all the letters of the alphabet, including big and small, as well as any numbers you want, the underscore symbol, and any combination of the above that you would like.

There are a few rules to remember that come with this one. First, you can't pick out a name that has a number at the front of it, or there is going to be an error. You also can't add in any spaces show up between the words that you want to write out. this means that you are not able to go with something like 5bears or 5 bears because they are going to show errors from the compiler. But you are able to write out something like fourkids and four_kids to help you name your identifier. Also, you want to make sure that you are not using up any of the keywords to name these.

When it comes to picking out the name that you would like to work with an identifier, make sure that you are able to remember what it is. it can follow all of the rules that we have listed above, but you will find that if you aren't able to remember the name that you gave to it, then it is going to be hard to execute the code and remember what you need to do with it later on. If you spell it in the wrong manner or you call it up under the wrong name, the compiler is not going to know what it is looking for and will send out an error message to you.

With these things in mind, if you pick out a name for the identifier that makes sense with what it is doing, and you make sure that the different rules that we have brought up are followed while naming then you shouldn't have any troubles when it comes to working with naming your identifiers.

FOCUSING ON THE CONTROL FLOW

When you work with the idea of any kind of coding language, you will need to pay attention to the control flow. The control flow is going to be there to ensure that the code is written out in the proper manner. There are a few strings in your code that you may want to write out so that the compiler is able to read them the right way. However, if you end up writing out the string in the wrong manner, you will see a few errors on the system. We will take a look at many codes in this guidebook to help you follow the right control flow for this kind of language, which can make it easier to know what you should get done, and how you are able to write out some of the codes with this language.

THE IDEA OF THE STATEMENTS

The next thing on the list that we need to take a look at is going to be the statements. You will find that you will work with a lot of statements when you are working with them in Python. These are just the strings of code that you need to write out, and that you would like the compiler to go through and write out on the screen for you.

When you tell the compiler the list of instructions that you want to work with it, you will find that those are the statements of your code. As long as you have been able to write them out properly, the compiler is going to read them and show up the kind of message that you want on the screen. The statements can be as short, or as long, as you would like, depending on the kind of code that you wish to write out.

THE COMMENTS

The next thing we are going to examine is the comments. There are going to be tied when you are writing out code in Python, and you will want to include an explanation or a note about what you are writing in this code. These notes aren't going to influence how the program works, and you don't want them to even be noticed by your program, but it can help you, and other programmers read the code and know better what is going on in the process.

It is pretty easy to add in these comments the way that you would like this language. You simply need to add the symbol of # ahead of the comment that you are writing. This is going to tell the compiler that you are working on one of these comments and the program, or the compiler is just going to avoid the comment and move on to the next part of the code.

As the coder, you are able to add in as many of these comments to the code as you would like to help explain out the code you are writing, and to keep things flowing nicely. It is actually possible to add one in every other line if you would like, though you want to keep these down a bit to just the ones that are most necessary for your code to work in the proper manner. But as long as you add in that # symbol to the front of the statement, you are able to add in any of these comments, and the compiler will know that you want it to just skip over that part.

LOOKING AT THE VARIABLES

Another part of the Python code that you need to work with is the variables. These are pretty common with most of the codes that you will write in Python, so it is important to learn them as much as possible The variables are going to be there to store some of the values that you need to keep track of and use in the code, and they can make sure that the different lines of the code are going to be organized and easy to read through.

Adding the value that you want to hit with the variables is going to be easy to do. You just need to place the equal space between the variables and whatever value you would like to assign to them, making sure that the compiler is going to know what it should do there. It is even possible to take this a bit further in order to get a few values to attach with the variables. If you would like, just add in the equal sign between each of them. If you take a look at some of the codes that we work with inside this guidebook, you will notice that there are a lot of variables found in the codes.

THE OPERATORS

The last basic part of the Python code that we need to take a look at here is the operators. These are going to be another simple option that you are able to work with, but you will notice that they are important that they can be in the codes that you write. You will find that there is actually a wide selection when it comes to working in the operators, and that allows you to really see some differences in how the code works.

For example, you will be able to work with the arithmetic operators to ensure that two parts of the code are going to be added together. You can do the comparison operators to help the programmer compare more than one part of the code together and see if they are the same or not. And you can work with the assigning operators to make sure that the right value is assigned to the right variable.

As we explored a bit with this chapter, there are a lot of different things that come with writing your own code in Python. The basics are meant to be simple so that you are able to really write out the codes that you need without a lot of hard stuff to start you out. There will be a lot more complicated stuff that we can add in later on, but for now, these are some great places to get started.

CHAPTER 3: PYTHON AS AN OOP LANGUAGE

One topic that we need to explore before we get too far into some of the codings with Python that we will do throughout this guidebook is the idea that Python is an object-oriented programming language or an OOP language. If you have looked into the ideas with the Python language in the past, then you may find that this is a term that you have seen in your search, even though you may have no idea what this is going to mean.

To help us understand what this OOP means, and why it is so important to understand how Python works, you will find that any language that is considered OOP is going to be easier to use, especially when it is compared to some of the coding languages that have been around for longer. With languages that are OOP, you see a coding language that wants to classify the classes and objects in a way that is easy to manipulate and work with. We will explore a bit about the classes later in this chapter, which is going to make understanding the OOP language a bit easier.

One feature that is nice to work with when you bring out the idea of an OOP language is that the procedures of any object you use are going to have some power in them to access fields of data, and even to ensure that you can make some modifications to them. With an OOP language, you will be able to design the program in any manner that you want, simply by working with the classes and the objects that are going to go into those classes.

This may seem like a simplistic manner to look at a coding language, and if you have stalled out on learning about a new coding language because you are worried about all of the challenges that are going to come with it, it is easy to feel that something is missing in the process. Or, it is possible that you see this simplicity and feel that the Python coding language, in particular, is not going to have the power that you would like for the programs that you would like to create.

Rest assured, though. You will find that OOP languages, even though they make things a bit easier, are still going to have all of the power that you need. Each language is going to be a bit different in how it is going to use this OOP part, but Python is going to be known as class-based. This means that the code is going to have the objects that you work with fit into a class. This ensures that things stay as organized as possible, and provides easy access to the things that you need when you need them.

You will quickly find that with a bit of practice with the Python code and its OOP functionality, you will be able to write programs with relative ease. If you have ever worked with some of the coding languages in the past, you may notice that some of the older ones are going to not be as organized or as easy to work with as the OOP with Python, and that may have turned you away from programming in the past. But OOP makes it easier and more possible for everyone, whether they are a beginner in coding or not, to do some of the programming's that they want.

Now, when you take a look at some of the features that are found in these OOP languages, you are going to be impressed. These languages are unique in that they are going to, for the most part, rely on the classes to ensure that they work well. In the next section, we will explore a bit more about what these classes are and how they are so powerful, but these ensure that the program is going to work the way that you would like.

Shared features that go with languages that are non-OOP. These languages are going to have some of the same features that are found with low-level features found in the older languages of coding. Some of the features that are still going to be available with the OOP languages like the Python code includes:

The variables: These variables are going to help you out by storing your formatted information inside a few different types of data. These are going to be built into the language and will include things like lists, tables, and strings.

Procedures: These come in with a lot of different names and you may see them called as functions or methods. These procedures are going to be able to take the input that your user provides and then will generate an output that you are able to use to manipulate the data that you have.

Classes and objects: We are soon going to take a bit closer look at the classes and objects, but these are going to be something important when it comes to an OOP language. These classes are going to be kind of like containers that are used to hold and store objects that tend to go with one another. This really adds a level of organization to your code that makes it easier to work with, and easier for the compiler to bring out what you need when you need it.

There are also going to be a few techniques and other structures found in these OOP languages that you need to learn about along the way to help you get some of the results that are needed. However, it is a good idea to look at some of the different features that are likely to show up with this kind of language overall, and are there to ensure that you are able to get the coding that you want to be done in a timely manner. Some of the best features that beginners enjoy when it comes to working with the OOP language include Encapsulation: You will find that when you work with an OOP language, you are going also to have a process that is known as encapsulation to help you. This is the process that has to come into place to bind data together. Any of the functions that are used for this kind of process are important because they are going to manipulate the data and ensure that it is secure from misuse within that code.

Dynamic dispatch and passing of messages. As you work to write some of your codes, you will find that there could be some external codes, but these are not going to be the ones in charge of selecting the procedural code when it is time to execute. This is something that is going to be passed over to the object. The object is going to do this by looking at the method that is associated with that object during run time in a process that is known as dynamic dispatch.

Open recursion: As you work through this OOP language, you may notice that it works with the idea of open recursion. This is basically when the object method is going to find itself called over with another method. You just need to use the keywords of this and self to help the process get going. These are going to be variables called late-bound, which means that they are going to let the method that has been defined in the class at hand invoke a method that you have placed in another class, or that you will define later on.

OOP languages are often a lot easier for coders to work with, especially when they have never been able to do any kind of coding in the past. As you work with a lot of the parts that come with the Python coding language, you will start to see more examples of this OOP feature, and see how it is able to make a big difference in how easy the code is to work with.

THE CLASSES AND THE OBJECTS

Now that we have brought up the idea of classes and objects through this chapter, it is time actually to explore these a bit and sees what they are all about. Both of these are going to be critical to making sure that the code will work the way that you want, and that all of the parts of your code show up at the time they are supposed to.

Basically, the classes are going to be the containers that show up in your code. They can be labeled anything that you would like, but often the name is going to have something to do with the objects that you place inside. The objects that are found in the same class need to go together in some manner. They don't have to all be exactly the same, but your goal is to have someone look inside the class and understand why the various objects are inside. With that introduction, let's dive a bit deeper into these classes and objects and see what they are all about and how they work.

CREATING YOUR OWN CLASSES

One thing that is important to learn how to work within the Python coding language is how to create these classes all on your own. The reason that we need to be able to do this is to add in some organization to the code and to make sure that various parts don't end up getting lost along the way. To make one of these classes, you need to be able to learn the keywords that are necessary to name a class.

The neat thing here is that you do get some freedom when you are naming the classes you create. You can give it pretty much any name that you want. But you should have it show up after the chosen keyword, and it works the best if it is given a name that is easy to remember at a later time.

Once you have taken the time to pick out the name that works the best for your class, it is time to name the subclass as well. This subclass is going to be found in the parenthesis of the code, so that makes it easier to find later if you need. Make sure that when this code is written out, and all of the parts have the name that you want to give them that there is a semicolon added to the end. This isn't a necessity, and if you forget it, your code should work just fine. But it is considered the right coding protocol to have it, so make sure to add it in to make things look nicer.

These classes are a simple idea, and it is pretty easy to bring them out and make them work for your needs. But now it is time to learn how to code with them and how to create some of the classes that are the best for your needs. Let's take a quick look at the kind of syntax that you need to work with to make this happen to create a class, and then we can divide the code up into smaller parts to show us how it goes together, and why the code is written the way that it is for creating classes.

```
class Vehicle(object):
#constructor
def_init_(self, steering, wheels, clutch, breaks, gears):
self._steering = steering
self._wheels = wheels
self._clutch = clutch
self._breaks =breaks
self._gears = gears
#destructor
def_del_(self):
    print("This is destructor....")

#member functions or methods
def Display_Vehicle(self):
    print('Steering:' , self._steering)
    print('Wheels:', self._wheels)
    print('Clutch:', self._clutch)
    print('Breaks:', self._breaks)
    print('Gears:', self._gears)
#instantiate a vehicle option
myGenericVehicle = Vehicle('Power Steering', 4, 'Super
Clutch', 'Disk Breaks', 5)
myGenericVehicle.Display_Vehicle()
```

Let's take some time to dissect this code to see what is all found inside of it. First, though, open up the compiler and add the code above into it to see what is going to happen. As you write it out, remember some of the different parts of the Python code that we talked about above, and see if you can recognize some of them in the code that we are writing.

Once that code is set up and ready to go, we need to take a look at the class definition that is part of this code. This class definition is going to be the part where you instantiate the object, and then you can add in the definition, so the object ends up going back to the class. This is important to note because it will make sure that the syntax is written into the code in the right manner.

When we are working on the class definition, you want to pay special attention because it is going to be responsible for telling your compiler what has to happen next. If you would like to make sure that you can set up a new definition of the class that you add to the code, the best function to use to make this happen includes object_attribute and object_method to help make it all come together.

Then we can move on and look at the second important part of the code above. We want to make sure that we are writing out the code in a way that is going to give your created class a special attribute. These special attributes will come into play because they give the coder a bit of peace of mind that your objects are going to end up in the right place of the code, and that everything will show up when you run the code, without a big mess.

The code that we wrote out before is going to show us a few examples of how these special attributes work. But there are a few additional special attributes that you may want to pull up and learn how to use as well. Some of the most common special attributes that are used in the Python code will include:

__bases__: this is considered a tuple that contains any of the superclasses

__module__: this is where you are going to find the name of the module, and it will also hold your classes.

__name__: this will hold on to the class name.

__doc__: this is where you are going to find the reference string inside the document for your class.

__dict__: this is going to be the variable for the dict. Inside the class name.

With this knowledge about special attributes in place, we also need to take some time to look at the best method to use to access a few of the members, or the objects, that you place into the class that you just created. You want to make sure that your compiler and your text editor are able to recognize the new class that you just created. If these are not able to find or recognize the new class that you were creating, then errors are going to start showing up in this part of the code when you reach it.

We, of course, want to make sure that the compiler is able to read the classes that we are setting up. To make this work, the code has to be set up the right way so that the compiler recognizes that we are creating a new class in the first place. Keep in mind that there are actually a few different methods that you are able to use when it comes to doing this, but the assessor method is often seen as the best one for this and is the easiest of the methods to use. An example of using this assessor method will include:

```python
class Cat(object)
    itsAge = None
    itsWeight = None
    itsName = None
    #set accessor function use to assign values to the fields
or member vars
    def setItsAge(self, itsAge):
    self.itsAge = itsAge

    def setItsWeight(self, itsWeight):
    self.itsWeight = itsWeight

    def setItsName(self, itsName):
    self.itsName =itsName

    #get accessor function use to return the values from a
field
    def getItsAge(self):
    return self.itsAge
    def getItsWeight(self):
    return self.itsWeight

    def getItsName(self):
    return self.itsName

objFrisky = Cat()
objFrisky.setItsAge(5)
objFrisky.setItsWeight(10)
objFrisky.setItsName("Frisky")
print("Cats Name is:", objFrisky.getItsname())
print("Its age is:", objFrisky.getItsAge())
print("Its weight is:", objFrisky.getItsName())
```

The classes that come with the Python coding language are not meant to be that complicated. In fact, they are there to make sure that the Python coding language is a bit easier to work with, especially when it is compared to some of the other coding languages, especially the ones that are a bit older. Learning how to create some of the classes in your code, along with how to place the objects into these new classes, will ensure that you will be able to write some of the best and most powerful codes that you need in the Python language.

CHAPTER 4: WRITING LOOPS IN PYTHON

The next thing that we need to take a look at when it is time to write some of your own codes in Python will be looped. Creating loops can help you to make a code that is more efficient, and will ensure that you are able to get codes written quickly and without a ton of work in the process. These loops work well with some of the conditional statements that we are going to talk about, later on, helping you to clear up your code while getting a lot done in a short amount of time.

Loops are helpful because they are going to speed up how long it is going to take you to write out some codes, can help to clean it all up, and can take hundreds of lines of code (potentially), and put it in just a few lines if needed. Think about how much time that is going to save when you can get all of that code into a few lines with the help of the loops.

If you are working on your code and you find that there are parts of the program that can repeat them over and over again, at least a few times, then the loops are going to help make this happen. You will be able to get the code to repeat as many times as you would like, without having to rewrite the same codes over and over again.

Let's say that you would like to work on some kind of program that has a multiplication table that is going to go from 1 to 10 and all of the answers that are needed for it. Maybe you would choose to do some of the beginner codes and write it all line by line while wasting a ton of time and making it so that the code looks kind of messy in the process. But you are able to use the idea of a lop and write it out with the help of a few lines. We will explore some of the different options that are available for the loops and using them, while also seeing how you would be able to do the example above in just a few lines.

While this may seem like a complex thing to work within the coding, it is actually pretty easy to work with, and even a beginner is going to be able to write out some of these codes. The way that these codes will work is that it tells the compiler to keep reading the same part of the code until there is some condition that is met. Once that condition is met, the compiler will get out of the loop and start working on the next part of the code.

So, let's say that you are working on a program, and a part of it needs to be able to count from one to ten. You would be able to use the idea of the loop in order to tell the compiler to keep going through the code until it reaches higher than ten. We can take a look at a few of the different examples that you are able to do with the ideas of the loop.

One thing to remember here is that when you write out some of these loops, it is important to set up the conditions in the right manner. It is easy to forget to set up these conditions when you first get started, but if you forget them right from the beginning of the code, then you will end up in a loop that is not going to stop. You will get stuck in a continuous loop because the code doesn't know when it needs to stop going through the loop.

When you decide to work with some of the methods that are considered more traditional with coding, or using some of the other methods that are found throughout this guidebook, your whole goal here will be to write out all of the lines of code to get things done. Even if you see some parts of the code repeating, then you would still need to rewrite it out. This could take a long time and may not be as easy to work with as well. But when you work with loops, this is not going to be something that is going to be that big of a deal.

When working with these loops, you are able to get rid of some of the traditional ways of coding and change it up and make things easier. You will be able to combine together a ton of lines of code, or as many as you would need in order to get things done. The compiler will still be able to read through it when the loop is done in the proper way, just as long as you make sure that all of your conditions are put in place.

Now that we have spent some time looking at what the loops mean and why they are going to be so important to your code writing, it is time to divide up some of the different types of loops that are available to help you get this done inside the codes you write.

THE FIRST LOOP: THE WHILE LOOP

So, the first type of loop that we are going to explore is the idea of the while loop in Python. This loop is a good one to bring out and use when you want to make sure that your code is able to go through the loop or the cycle for a predetermined number of times. You can pick out how many times you would like the code to go through this kind of loop to get the best results out of it. This makes it easy to get the number of times you would like the loop to go through.

When you work with the while loop, the goal is not to make the code that you write go through the cycle an indefinite amount of times. But you do have in mind a number of times that you would like the code to do its work. So, if you want to count from one to ten in the code, your goal is to use the while loop in order to go through the loop that many times.

With the while loop, you will see that the code is going to go through the loop, and then it will double check to see if the conditions are met or not. Then, if the conditions are not met, they will go through the loop again and then check again. It will continue doing this over and over again until it has met the conditions, and then it will go on to the other part of the code when the loop is all gone.

To see how the while loop is going to work, and to gain a better understanding of the loop works in general, let's look at some examples of a code that has a while loop inside of it:

```
counter = 1
while(counter <= 3):
    principal = int(input("Enter the principal amount:"))
    numberofyeras = int(input("Enter the number of years:"))
    rateofinterest = float(input("Enter the rate of interest:"))
    simpleinterest = principal * numberofyears * rateofinterest/100
    print("Simple interest = %.2f" %simpleinterest)
    #increase the counter by 1
    counter = counter + 1
    print("You have calculated simple interest for 3 times!")
```

Before we take a look at some of the other types of loops that we are able to work with, let's open up the compiler on Python and type in the code to see what is going to happen when we execute it. You will then be able to see how the while loop is able to work. The program is able to go through and figure out the interest rates, along with the final amounts that are associated with it, based on the numbers that the user, or you, will put into the system.

With the example from the code that was above, we have the loop set up so that it is going to go through three times. This means that the user gets a chance to put in different numbers and see the results three times, and then the system will be able to move on. You do get the chance to add in more or take out some loops based on what is the best for your needs.

THE SECOND LOOP: THE FOR LOOP

At this point, we have been able to take a look at the while loop and what it is all going to entail, it is time to take a look at the for loop so that we are able to see how this in order to do more with loops, and how this is going to be different than the while loop overall. When you work with the while loops, you will notice that the code is going to go through a loop a certain number of times. But it is not always going to work for all of the situations

- 65 -

where you want to bring in a loop. And the for loop is going to help us to fill in the blanks that the while loop is not able to do.

When you are ready to work with the for loop, you will be able to set up the code in a manner that the user isn't going to be the one who will go into the code and provide the program with the information that it needs. They do not have the control that is needed to stop the loop from running.

Instead of the user being able to hold the control, the for loop is going to be set up so that it will go over the iteration of your choice in the order that you place the items into your code. This information, when the for loop is going to list them out in the exact way that they are listed in the code. The user will not need to input anything for the for loop to work.

A good example of how this is going to work inside your code so that you are able to make it work for your needs will include the following syntax:

```
# Measure some strings:
words = ['apple,' 'mango,' 'banana,' 'orange']
for w in words:
print(w, len(w))
```

When you work with the for loop example that is above, you are able to add it to your compiler and see what happens when it gets executed. When you do this, the four fruits that come out on your screen will show up in the exact order that you have them written out. If you would like to have them show up in a different order, you can do that, but then you need to go back to your code and rewrite them in the right order, or your chosen order. Once you have then written out in the syntax and they are ready to be executed in the code, you can't make any changes to them.

THE THIRD LOOP: THE NESTED LOOP

The third and final loop that we are going to work within Python is going to be known as the nested loop. You will find that when we look at the nested loop, there are going to be some parts that are similar to what we looked at with the while loop and with the for loop, but it is going to use these topics in a different way. when you decide to work with a nested loop, you will just take one loop, and then make sure that it is placed inside of another loop. Then, both of these loops will work together and continue on with their work until both have had a chance to finish.

This may seem really hard to work with when it comes to the loops, and you may wonder if there is actually any time that you, as a beginner, would need to work with this loop. But there are often a lot more chances to work with the nested loop than you may think in the beginning. For example, if you are working some kind of code that needs to have a multiplication table inside of it, and you want the answers listed all the way up, then you are going to work with the nested loop.

Imagine how long this kind of process is going to take if you have to go out and list each and every part of the code without using a loop to make it happen. You would have to write out the lines of codes to do one time one, one's times two, and so on until you reach the point where you are at ten times ten. This would end up being a ton of lines of code just to make this kind of table work in your code. But you are able to work with the idea of the nested loop in order to see the results that you want.

A good example that you will be able to work with to show how a nested loop works and to make sure that you are able to make a full multiplication table of your own, includes the following:

#write a multiplication table from 1 to 10
For x in xrange(1, 11):
        For y in xrange(1, 11):
        Print '%d = %d' % (x, y, x*x)

When you got the output of this program, it is going to look similar to this:

1*1 = 1
1*2 = 2
1*3 = 3
1*4 = 4

All the way up to 1*10 = 2

Then it would move on to do the table by twos such as this:

2*1 =2
2*2 = 4

And so on until you end up with 10*10 = 100 as your final spot in the sequence.

Go ahead and put this into the compiler and see what happens. You will simply have four lines of code, and end up with a whole multiplication table that shows up on your program. Think of how many lines of code you would have to write out to get this table the traditional way that you did before? This table only took a few lines to accomplish, which shows how powerful and great the nested loop can be.

As you can see, there are a lot of different things that you are able to do when you start to implement some loops into the codes that you are writing. There are a ton of reasons why you should add a loop into the code you are writing. You will be able to use it in most cases to take a large amount of code and write it in just a few lines instead. This saves you time, cleans up the code that you are trying to light, and the compiler is going to be able to still help you do some things that are super powerful!

CHAPTER 5: CONDITIONAL STATEMENTS

```
17   string sInput;
18   int iLength, iN;
19   double dblTemp;
20   bool again = true;
21
22   while (again) {
23       iN = -1;
24       again = false;
25       getline(cin, sInput);
26       system("cls");
27       stringstream(sInput) >> dblTemp;
28       iLength = sInput.length();
29       if (iLength < 4) {
30           again = true;
31           continue;
32       } else if (sInput[iLength - 3] != '.') {
33           again = true;
34           continue;
35       } while (++iN < iLength) {
         if (isdigit(sInput[iN])) {
             continue;
         } else if (iN == (iLength - 3) ) {
         } else if (iN
             ...nue;
```

Another fun topic that we get to spend some time working with when it comes to the Python language is the idea of conditional statements. These are also called the if statements in some cases, or even the decision statements. Learning how to use these will basically teach your computer how to react to the input from the user, even if you are not there to control what is going on.

There are going to be some times in your coding when you will want the program to be able to make some decisions or do some actions on its own, based on what the user tells it, without you needing to go through and code in every piece of the puzzle. Any time that the user is allowed to put in an answer that is all their own, rather than having to pick out from a selection of answers that you provide, then you are working with the decision control statements, or the conditional statements, to make this happen.

There are a few varieties when it comes to working with these kinds of statements, and the one that you go with will be based on what you are trying to do with the code. You can work with the if statement, the if else statement, and the elif statements.

The first option here that we are going to take a look at is known as the if statement. These are going to be pretty simple to work with, and there is not necessarily a lot of power that is behind them. But they will work on the idea that the answer that you get from the user is either seen as true or as false. If it is true, the program will continue on, and if the answer is seen as false, then the program will stop.

You can imagine already that there is going to be a bit of a problem with using the if statement in a lot of cases, and this is why you may not see it all that often. But it is still a good option to start out with when you are learning how these conditional statements are going to work. A good example of how you will be able to use the if statement will be the following:

age = int(input("Enter your age:"))
if (age <=18):
     print("You are not eligible for voting, try next election!")
print("Program ends")

Let's explore what is going to happen with this code when you put it into your program. If the user comes to the program and puts that they are younger than 18, then there will be a message that shows up on the screen. In this case, the message is going to say "You are not eligible for voting, try next election!" Then the program, as it is, is going to end. But what will happen to this code if the user puts in some age that is 18 or above?

With the if statement, nothing will happen if the user says that their age is above 18. The if statement just has one option and will focus on whether the answer that the user provides is going to match up with the conditions that you set with your code. The user has to put in that they are under the age of 18 with the if statement in this situation, or you won't be able to get the program to happen again.

As we mentioned a bit before, there are going to be times when the if statement could cause some problems. You naturally want the user to put in their actual age when they join the program, rather than only putting in the right answers. And if nothing shows up in your program when the user puts in the wrong age, this is going to leave them with something that makes no sense, or even a program that ends. It's likely that this is not what you want to work with.

This is where the if else statements are going to start showing up, and you will quickly find that they are more useful to work with than the plain if statements. The if else statements are going to work with the idea that we just did and then takes it a step further. The point with the if else statement is to make sure that the program does something, no matter what answer they are able to give to the program.

Going with the idea of the example that we talked about above, you may want to go through and separate the people out into two groups. You may have a group who is 18 and under, and a group that is over 18 years old. This is something that the if else statement is going to be able to help you work with, and will ensure that, no matter what answer the user adds in for their age, something comes up. A good example of the code that you are able to use when it is time to bring in the if else statements include:


```
age = int(input("Enter your age:"))
if (age <=18):
        print("You are not eligible for voting, try next election!")
else
        print("Congratulations! You are eligible to vote. Check out your local polling station to find out more information!)
print("Program ends")
```


As you can see, this really helps to add some more options to your code and will ensure that you get an answer no matter what results the user gives to you. You can also change up the message to say anything that you want, but the same idea will be used no matter the answer that the user gives.

The example above is going to be a pretty simple one to work with. You can add in as many possibilities to the if else statements as you would like and you do not have to limit yourself to just two options as we did above. If you only need to work with two options, then this is fine to stick with. But there are lots of codes that need to expand to more, and the if else statement is going to help with that as well.

For example, maybe you want to split the individuals who come to your program into five different age groups rather than just the two from before. You can just go through and add in an if part of the statement, along with a message that you would like to go with it and continue on with the if else statements. You can technically add in as many options as you would like based on the kind of code that you are trying to develop.

Another example of using the if else statement is when you are creating a program that wants the person to pick out their favorite type of drink. There are a lot of options out there when it comes to tasty drinks, and you can definitely expand out the if else statements. Maybe you pick out a few options like pop, milk, juice, and coffee. Then you can add in the else statement that is going to be your "catch-all" in case the user decides to pick water or something else as their favorite drink. When this is in place, no matter what answer the user gives to the program there will be some kind of result that shows up.

Adding a catch-all to the end of your code, or the "else" part of this, can be important. You can't always think about all the different examples that the person may put in. You could put a hundred options into your code (which would take a lot of time and be messy and not really necessary), and then the user will name a color differently or pick the one color that you forgot. If you don't have that as an option, then the program won't know how to behave from there.

The else statement here is important because it helps you to catch all of the remaining answers that the user could give you. If you don't have a statement in the code to handle the answer that the user gives, then the else statement will make sure to get you covered. Just make sure that you have that else statement in place to get it done.

THE ELIF STATEMENTS

We have spent some time talking about two of the conditional statements that are available for Python coding. The first ones, the if statements are a good place to start to get some practice with the conditional statements. They are based on the idea of the answer the user giving you is true or false. If the user gives an answer that is seen as true, then the program will finish up what you have next in the code. If the answer is seen as something false, then the program is going to end. It is meant to be something that is simple to work with and can give you some practice with writing codes.

Then you can move on to the if else statements if your code needs something a bit more to it. With the if else statements, we took this a bit further and set up something that is going to make sure that the user is going to get some kind of results, no matter what answer they put into the system. We even looked at a few examples of how you would be able to use the if else statement so we can see how they are different compared to the if statements.

And the third type of conditional statement that you can work with when you want to code in Python is known as the elif statement. The elif statement is going to be great to work with because it allows the user to look at a few options that you can present them with, and then, based on the kind of answer that the user gives, the program is going to execute the results that you added into the code for it.

You will actually see a lot of different programs that are going to rely on the elif statements. One place where you may see this kind of conditional statement is when you play a game, and there is a menu that starts up on the program then this is a good sign that an elif statement is being used. These conditional statements are going to be useful when it comes to providing a few options to the user, rather than one or two.

When you use the elif statements, you get a bit of freedom with what you are going to add into the code. You can choose to add in just a few options, or you can add in quite a bit, as long as you write this code out in the right way and you double check that the right function is put in the right place. In addition, you may want to keep the number of these that you use to a minimum because having too many is going to add some complexity to the code. You have to decide if this is what you would like to do.

One of the best ways to determine how to use the elif statements and whether it is going to work in the code that you are trying to write is to look at some examples of how the elif statement works. The following syntax can be used to write an elif statement:

```
if expression1:
statement(s)
elif expression2:
statement(s)
elif expression3:
statement(s)
else:
statement(s)
```

This is a pretty basic syntax of the elif statement and you can add in as many of these statements as you would like. Just take that syntax and then place the right information into each part and the answer that is listed next to it. Notice that there is also an else statement at the end of this. Don't forget to add this to your code so that it can catch any answer that the user puts in that isn't listed in your elif statements.

To help you better understand how these elif statements work and how the syntax above is going to work, let's take a look at a little game that you can create using these statements:

```
Print("Let's enjoy a Pizza! Ok, let's go inside Pizzahut!")
print("Waiter, Please select Pizza of your choice from the
menu")
pizzachoice = int(input("Please enter your choice of
Pizza:"))
if pizzachoice == 1:
        print('I want to enjoy a pizza napoletana')
elif pizzachoice == 2:
        print('I want to enjoy a pizza rustica')
elif pizzachoice == 3:
        print('I want to enjoy a pizza capricciosa')
else:
        print("Sorry, I do not want any of the listed pizza's,
please bring a Coca Cola for me.")
```

When you add this into your code, the user is going to have the
benefit of going through this part of the program and making
the choice based on what they want. And if you get it set up the
proper way, you will have the right answer come up for them.
So, if the user decides that they would like to choose the pizza
rustica, they would need to go through and select number 2. If
they want to have just a drink and none of the pizza options that
are listed, then they would click on that.

Remember you are able to add in as many options as you would
like to the conditional statements of the elif statement. It is all
about what works the best for your program. You may have four

options, or you can have twenty, but try to keep these to just the ones that your program needs to function in the proper manner for your needs.

As you can see here, the conditional statements are going to work well to help you gain more power in your codes, and they will help you to get the program to work, even if you are not able to guess all of the answers that someone is going to give you in the program. It allows the program to make some of the decisions without you while ensuring that your code is going to behave while the user is interacting with it. Make sure to try out some of the examples of conditional statements in the compiler to see how these work and to get more familiar with the way that you are able to use these.

CHAPTER 6: RAISING AN EXCEPTION

We have spent some time looking at some of the different things that you are able to work on when you bring out the Python code. Now it is time to bring up a new idea of what you are able to do, which is to raise exceptions. We need to focus on how to raise some of your own exceptions in the codes that you write, as well as how to handle any exceptions that the computer program decides to raise on its own.

The more that you work with coding in Python, you will find that the program is going to bring out some of its own exceptions as you go. There are a few exceptions that are part of the Python code, so it is able to behave in the manner that you want it too. But then there is also a chance when you will purposely add into the program so that it raises an exception and behaves the way that you would like.

The ones that the program is going to raise on its own will be automatic because they are already placed into the Python library. A good example of this one is when the user tries to divide by zero in the code. The Python library is set up not to let this happen so it will raise the exception for you. On the other hand though, if there is a new exception that you would like to work with that is just for your own program that you are working on. You can rise up an exception to work with any kind of program that you want.

As the programmer here, you will want to learn how to work with all of the exceptions that are found within the Python library. When you know how these exceptions work, it is easier to add what you need into the code, and you can even learn when the exceptions will start to turn up for you. While there are a lot of exceptions that are out there, some of the most common exceptions and the keywords that come with the Python code include:

Finally—this is the action that you will want to use to perform cleanup actions, whether the exceptions occur or not.

Assert—this condition is going to trigger the exception inside of the code

Raise—the raise command is going to trigger an exception manually inside of the code.

Try/except—this is when you want to try out a block of code and then it is recovered thanks to the exceptions that either you or the Python code raised.

HOW TO RAISE AN EXCEPTION IN YOUR CODE

The first thing that we need to take a look at when we learn about exceptions inside of code is how we can use them. When those automatic exceptions start to show up, it is important to be prepared and learn how you can take some steps to make the exceptions make more sense.

So, when you work on your code, and you see that there is an issue or an exception that starts to show up, or you want to figure out why it seems that your program is doing something that seems off, you can look and see whether or not your compiler is raising a new exception. These are going to be raised when the code is looking through your work and can't figure out what steps it should take next to make the program work the way that you want.

The good news is that many times, the issues that come up with these exceptions are going to be simple and easy to fix. For example, it could be something as simple as trying to call up a file, but you misspelled a word or called it the wrong thing, either when you are calling it up or when you saved it. The compiler won't be able to find the file because it is not all matching up, but you can just go back in and fix that problem in a few seconds and get the best results.

Let's take a look at how you are able to make these exceptions work. The best way to understand how exceptions are going to work and make sure we understand what it is going to look like when the compiler decides to raise an exception is to do an example of our own. The following is a simple exception that we can use to study for this endeavor:


```
x = 10
y = 10
result = x/y #trying to divide by zero
print(result)
```

The output that you are going to get when you try to get the interpreter to go through this code would be:


```
>>>
Traceback (most recent call last):
      File "D: \Python34\tt.py", line 3, in <module>
      result = x/y
ZeroDivisionError: division by zero
>>>
```

Taking a look at the example that is above, you will see that the compiler will try to read through it and will bring up an error for you. The only reason that this happens is that you or the user is trying to divide by zero at some point. You have a few options from this point. You can either leave things the way that they are and run the program in the manner that it is now, which provides you with an error message that is kind of messy and hard to read. Or you can make some changes to determine exactly what that message should be saying to the user.

For most programmers, it is agreed that you should try to change up the error message at least a bit. This helps to eliminate the messy message that no one really understands, and makes it easier for the user to understand why they are getting the error message in the first place. When the exception is raised, you do not want the user to be confused as to what they should do next, or they may get frustrated and not want to use the program any longer. Raising an exception and making sure that you have it organized the right way will make your user enjoy the program that much more. A good example of how to clean up the exceptions a bit will include the following:

```
x = 10
y = 0
result = 0
try:
        result = x/y
        print(result)
except ZeroDivisionError:
        print("You are trying to divide by zero.")
```

As you can see, the code that we just put into the compiler is going to be pretty similar to the one that we wrote above. But we did go through and change up the message to show something there when the user raises this exception. When they do get this exception, they will see the message "You are trying to divide by zero" come up on the screen. This isn't a necessary step, but it definitely makes your code easier to use!

HOW TO DEFINE YOUR OWN EXCEPTIONS

With the examples that we did above, we were focusing on how we could raise an exception based on what is seen as an error or an issue with the Python library. But now we need to take this a bit further and see what else we can do. You will be able to use Python in order to create some of your own codes along the way, which design your own programs as well. And there may be times when you want to change up the rules and have an exception raised based on what is allowed and what is not allowed for your program.

These exceptions are not going to be ones found in the Python library. And that is just fine. But because of this, you need to be able to write out the code in a manner that allows it to bring up that exception because the Python library is not going to do it for you at all.

For example, you may be working on your own program, and you decide that when your user is on it, they should only be able to add in certain numbers to the code, and the others are going to be wrong. This may work best when you decide to create a program or a game to play. Or you could have it so that an exception comes up if you only want the user to have a chance to answer the question three times rather than them doing it an indefinite number of times. If they get it right, then the program would go on. If they get it wrong, then the exception will be raised after the third time.

These kinds of exceptions may not be found in the Python library, but they are going to be important to how well the program can work and the results that you will be able to get from them. And they can ensure that the program you are writing, no matter what kind of program it is, will work in the proper manner. A good example of the code that you can write out to make this happen will include:

```
class CustomException(Exception):
def_init_(self, value):
      self.parameter = value
def_str_(self):
      return repr(self.parameter)
try:
      raise CustomException("This is a CustomError!")
except CustomException as ex:
      print("Caught:", ex.parameter)
```

When you finish this particular code, you are done successfully adding in your own exception. When someone does raise this exception, the message "Caught: This is a CustomError!" will come up on the screen. You can always change the message to show whatever you would like, but this was there as a placeholder to show what we are doing. Take a moment here to add this to the compiler and see what happens.

In the beginning, it may seem like exception handling is going to be a bit silly and like it is not worth your time to learn how to use this at all. You may assume that only certain kinds of programs are going to work well with these exceptions and that anything else is just a waste of time to learn this.

However, you may be surprised at how often you would need to bring these exceptions up for your needs. Even in programs that are not too complex, or in programs that don't really need the exception to be raised in the first place, there can be some benefit to using them, and learning how to change up the message, as well as raise some of your own along the way. it is definitely something that you should learn how to do well when you decide to write your own codes in the Python language.

As you start to work on your codes more and try to make them a bit more advanced in Python, you will notice that raising exceptions is something that will become pretty common to you. There are a lot of times that you can work with exceptions, whether you are working on some that are unique to your own program, or some that are recognized by the Python library on its own.

Working with some of the codes and examples that we explored in this chapter will ensure that you are well on your way to seeing some great success with exceptions and that you will be able to make these work well for your needs. It may take a bit of time to learn, but adding these to your compiler, and getting some practice, can be a great way to help you out!

Chapter 7: The Beauty of Inheritances in the Python Language

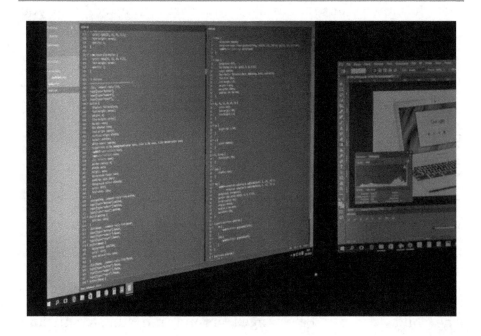

There are a lot of different things that you are able to work on when you decide to add Python into the mix. You will be able to write some awesome codes along the way, and even as a beginner you are going to find that you can write codes to do anything that you would like. But now we are going to focus a bit on how you can write out inheritances in Python and why it is such an important part of the Python code.

Inheritances are a nice addition to your skills with Python because they will ensure that you can write out some complex parts of the code, without having to rewrite it a bunch of times. This helps to not only clean up the code and make it look nicer but can also make writing out the code a bit easier overall as well. It allows you to reuse a specific part of the code that you need, without having to rewrite it.

To help make the idea of how inheritances work a bit easier to understand, you have to remember that this type of coding is going to take an original code, one that you already wrote out earlier, and copy it down to make up a new part of the code that is based on the first one. The first part of this is going to be called the parent code, and the second part is going to be the child code.

The child code can be changed around and adjusted in any manner that you want, and there will be no changes to the parent code when you do this. This allows you a bit more freedom with what you are working on and ensures that this is going to behave the way that you want. You can also make as many of these children codes as you would like based on what needs to happen to make your code work properly.

While this may, at first, sound a bit complicated, inheritances are pretty easy to learn. You will have to go through a few steps to make it happen, and it may look like a lot of code, but it ends up being a lot less than what you would see if you just rewrote the code rather than using the inheritance all of the time. A good example of how these inheritances can work will include the following:

```
#Example of inheritance
#base class
class Student(object):
      def __init__(self, name, rollno):
      self.name = name
      self.rollno = rollno
#Graduate class inherits or derived from Student class
class GraduateStudent(Student):
      def __init__(self, name, rollno, graduate):
      Student __init__(self, name, rollno)
      self.graduate = graduate
def DisplayGraduateStudent(self):
      print"Student Name:", self.name)
      print("Student Rollno:", self.rollno)
      print("Study Group:", self.graduate)
#Post Graduate class inherits from Student class
class PostGraduate(Student):
      def __init__(self, name, rollno, postgrad):
      Student __init__(self, name, rollno)
      self.postgrad = postgrad
```

```python
    def DisplayPostGraduateStudent(self):
    print("Student Name:", self.name)
    print("Student Rollno:", self.rollno)
    print("Study Group:", self.postgrad)
#instantiate from Graduate and PostGraduate classes
    objGradStudent = GraduateStudent("Mainu", 1,
"MS-Mathematics")
    objPostGradStudent = PostGraduate("Shainu", 2,
"MS-CS")
    objPostGradStudent.DisplayPostGraduateStudent(
)
```

When you type this into your interpreter, you are going to get the results:

```
('Student Name:', 'Mainu')
('Student Rollno:', 1)
('Student Group:', 'MSC-Mathematics')
('Student Name:', 'Shainu')
('Student Rollno:', 2)
('Student Group:', 'MSC-CS')
```

As a coder, you will find that these inheritances are going to help you gain some freedom when you write out the codes. If you are able to take a parent class or the base class, and you want to make sure that it works later on with your child or derived class, the inheritance is going to ensure that you are able to do this while keeping the features of the parent class that you want, and kicking out the features that won't work for you. Add in that you can also add in some new things if needed to the child class, and you can see why the inheritances are going to be a great option for you.

As you work with the inheritances, remember that you have the freedom to add in as many of the derived classes as you want from the original base class. As long as you make sure that they are done in the order that you need them to, such as what we did with the example above, you will be able to have as many of these derived classes as are needed to get the work done. And you can even change up each level of this to end up with the results that you want along the way.

HOW TO OVERRIDE MY BASE CLASS

The next thing that we need to take a look at when we look at inheritances is the idea of overriding one of the base classes that you have. There are going to be times when you have a class that is derived, and you would like to take the right steps that are needed to override things that are found in the base class. This means that you will see the base class and then change up some of the behavior that is inside of it. This is going to ensure that you are able to create a base class that has the behavior that you want from the derived class, along with some other behaviors that are needed in your code.

It may sound like this is going to add in too much complexity to the process, but it is a great way to give you the power to control which parental features you would like to have shown up in your derived class when you create it. This will be the easiest way for you to make sure that the right features end up in your new class while maintaining some of the parental features that you want as well in that class.

TRYING OUT SOME OVERLOADING

In addition to being able to override the base class and get some of the other options sorted out and ready to go, you can also use a process with your inheritances that are known as overloading. When you decide to work with overloading, you will take one of the identifiers and use it to help define two or more methods at a time. For most cases, there are going to be no more than two methods in the class, but sometimes this number can go a bit higher.

The two methods that you want to use with overloading need to be found in the same class. They will have parameters that are different, so make sure they come with different processes. Overloading will then work for you when you have them do a task that has to be done under the different parameters.

Overloading is a bit more complex to work with than what most beginners will need. But as you explore more of what can be done with the Python language over time, and you work on more codes, you are sure to run across times when it is needed.

A FINAL NOTE CONCERNING INHERITANCES

As you are working on a variety of codes in Python, you may come across times when one inheritance is not enough, and you will want to write out several at a time. This process is known as multiple inheritances, and when you do this, you will find that each level is going to have some similarities to one another, but each level can still allow for some smaller changes. You can just keep going doing the line, repeating the steps that you did in the example before.

When you start to do some codes that need multiple inheritances, you will take one class, also known as your base class, and you will give it at least two parent classes to get started. This is an important thing to learn when you are growing your code because you can really help to use it to get the code written out as long as you need.

Multiple inheritances can be as simple or as complicated as you would like to make them. When you work on them, you will be able to create a brand new class, which we will call Class C, and you got the information to create this new class from the previous one, or Class B. Then you can go back and find that Class B was the one that you created from information out of Class A. Each of these layers is going to contain some features that you like from the class ahead of it, and you can go as far into it as you would like. Depending on the code that you decide to write, you could have ten or more of these classes, each level having features from the previous one to keep it going.

When you decide to create one of the multiple inheritances, remember that while you can keep going down the line and making as many derived classes as you would like, the circular inheritance is not allowed. You can add in as much of the parent class that the derived classes need to code, but you can't go around and make a circle connect things with this kind of method.

As you get more into the Python code and you write some of your own codes in the process, you will find that working with all of these inheritances can be popular because they help to keep the code organized and neat. There are a lot of times when you are able to reuse the same block of code throughout the program, with just a few changes, while saving your time and your fingers from rewriting all of those codes again.

CHAPTER 8: THE REGULAR EXPRESSIONS

The next type of coding skill that we are going to take a look at is known as a regular expression. When you work with the Python coding language, one thing that you will notice is the library that comes with it. This library is going to contain a lot of different options including regular expressions, which can help you handle all of your searches while making sure that the right actions happen behind the scenes as well.

These expressions are important because they help the compiler help you filter out different texts or strings of texts. It is possible for you to use this in order to check and see if a text or some string of text is found in the code you are working with and then match it back up to the regular expression as you see fit. When you are ready to write out some of your regular expressions it is possible to stick with a syntax that is similar each time, no matter what option you are using. It even works in other languages so even if you go from Python to another coding language, you will use the same syntax.

Now, you may be reading through this and have some questions about what regular expressions really are and how you would be able to use them to get things to work out well with your codes. A good place for us to start with this is to bring out our text editor and have the program try to locate a word, one that was spelled out in different manners in the same code. We will take a look at a few ways that you can do this with regular expressions so that this makes a bit more sense as you go through.

You will find that there are a lot of times when you will be able to use regular expressions when writing Python codes. This is why it is so important for us to figure out how to write them. The first step to consider when you want to work with the regular expressions is to import the expression library. This often happens when you first start up your Python program to see if it did that for you or not. You should get in the habit of doing this though because you will use it on a regular basis.

When it is time to work on writing some statements in Python, you will often need to bring up some regular expressions. As soon as you know all that the regular expressions are able to help you to do, you will see a lot of power show up in some of the codes that you write. Let's explore a bit about how the regular expressions work, how they can be used in your codes, and how you are able to work to make them perform the way that you want in the code.

LOOKING AT THE BASIC PATTERNS WITH REGULAR EXPRESSIONS

The first thing that we have to explore when we are working with regular expressions is that they are available to use in a lot of different kinds of equations and characters, rather than just one kind. This is going to make it easier for you to watch for some of the patterns that are going to show up when you need them. As you work with regular expressions, you will start to see that there are a few patterns that are pretty common and will show up often with these and they include:

a, X, 9, < -- ordinary characters just match themselves exactly. The meta-characters that aren't going to match themselves simply because they have a special meaning include: . ^ $ * ? { [] and more.

. (the period)—this is going to match any single except the new line symbol of '\n'

3. \w—this is the lowercase w that is going to match the "word" character. This can be a letter, a digit, or an underbar. Keep in mind that this is the mnemonic and that it is going to match a single word character rather than the whole word.

\b—this is the boundary between a non-word and a word.

\s—this is going to match a single white space character including the form, form, tab, return, newline, and even space. If you do \S, you are talking about any character that is not a white space.

^ = start, $ = end—these are going to match to the end or the start of your string.

\t, \n, \r—these are going to stand for tab, newline, and return

\d—this is the decimal digit for all numbers between 0 and 9. Some of the older regex utilities will not support this so be careful when using it

\ --this is going to inhibit how special the character is. If you use this if you are uncertain about whether the character has some special meaning or not to ensure that it is treated just like another character.

Of course, these are not the limits of the regular expression that you can add into your code, but they are some of the most common ones that you are going to rely on as a beginner. There are a lot of different codes where you are going to need them, and it is possible that you will want to bring in more than one regular expression in the mix.

DOING A QUERY WITH YOUR REGULAR EXPRESSIONS

In addition to doing some of the work as we did above to find the basic patterns in your Python code, it is possible to bring out the regular expressions to help you to do a search on any of the input strings in the code. The neat thing with this one is that there are going to be several methods that you can use for this, based on what you are looking for in the code.

Every time that you are ready to do a query, you may find that you need to do something a bit different based on what you want to get out of the process. Working with regular expressions on the Python code will make sure that you are able to pick out the right queries to get things done. Let's look at three of the most common query results that you are able to use when working on a Python code.

THE SEARCH METHOD

The first of the three query methods that we are going to work with is known as the search() method. This is a good one to rely on because it will let you match up a text or a string of text to another one, no matter where it ends up in the code. This function isn't going to come with a lot of restrictions like you may see with the other two. It is going to work the best when you want to be able to search through the whole string of text for the answer, rather than just the end of the string.

This means that the search method is going to be able to look inside a string of text and find whether something is there or not, no matter where this match is going to show up. A good example of how you can use the search method includes:

```
import re
string = 'apple, orange, mango, orange'
match = re.search(r'orange', string)
print(match.group(0))
```

Take a moment to add this to your compiler and see what output you get. This code is going to give you an output of "orange". With this method, you are only going to see the match one time.

There could be ten oranges in the code, the search function will just tell you if one is there, not how many of that item are in the string. Even though there are technically two oranges in the code above, the search() method will just return one of them to you. Once it finds that first orange, it has done its job and will stop. Later we will discuss another method that you can use that can help you know exactly how many of an item are in the string.

THE MATCH METHOD

There are a lot of times when you will be able to bring out the search method and make it work in your code, but there are also other types of queries that you will want to work with. And the second type of query that we are going to look at is the match method. This one is going to find the matches again, but it will only check to see if the match is found at the beginning of your string, rather than anywhere in the string. It is the best query to work with for looking for a specific pattern inside the syntax that you are searching for.

We can see how the match method is going to be different by comparing it to the search method from before. You can see that there is a pattern, where the object "orange' is going to show up alternating with the other words there. but when you work with the match function, you would switch out the research with the re_match instead. In this case, based on how the pattern is right now, you are not going to get any results because the word orange is not the first one in the string of text.

Even though you can see that orange is in the code, it is not going to be the first part of the string. In what we have written out, Apple is going to be the first word in this string. The match method is just looking to see if there is a match between the first word or not, and since orange is not going to be that first word, it is not going to show up.

You can always change around the order of the words that are found inside of the code, you will be able to really get it to work out the way that you want. But the match method is only going to compare the search term with the first term that is in your string of text.

THE FINDALL METHOD

And the third query option that we can work with when it comes to the regular expressions will be the findall method. With the other two methods, you will just find out whether the object you are trying to match will show up in the string, either anywhere in the string or at the beginning of the string. But the findall method is going to be a bit different. This one tells you how many times the object is going to show up inside your string of text in the first place. So, if we use the option from before, you will use the findall method and get the result of "orange, orange". Since there is two present, this is going to give you two options to work with.

You are going to have some options here because there can be as many of the same object in the string as needed, or you can pick out another kind of object as well. If you added twenty oranges into this, the findall method would list out orange twenty times when you used it. Or, if you change this and try to look up apple you would only get one apple back as a result here.

Try out the final method and find out how it is different compared to the search and the match method that we worked with. You can just type in the code from the compiler that we had before and change out the method that you are working with. Add some things, take some things away, and then see how these three are going to work with each other. This is the best way to get used to working with the query options when it comes to regular expressions.

Chapter 9: What is Scikit-Learn and Other Libraries That Work Well with Python?

Now that we have had some time to look through the Python code and some of the different things that we are able to do with this code. There are a number of libraries that you are able to work with when it comes to Python, which is going to make it even easier to do some of the different codes that you would like to work with.

You can easily just work with the regular kind of library that comes with Python, which gives you a lot of freedom and you will be able to use them in order to handle the codes that we have been looking at in this guidebook. But there are times when you will want to work with a different kind of library based on what is going to happen with the code you are writing. For example, if you want to work with machine learning, the Scikit-Learn library is going to be a good option to look at.

There are a lot of different libraries that you are able to work with based on what you want to do with your coding. But the main libraries that we are going to look at will include Numpy, Matplotlib, Scipy, and Scikit-Learn.

NUMPY

The first Python library that we are going to take a look at is NumPy. This is a good library to work with that helps to add in some more support as needed for large and multi-dimensional arrays and matrices. It is also going to include a bigger collection of high-level mathematical functions so that you can actually use your codes to operate these arrays. The original ancestor library that came before this one, known as Numeric, was created by Jim Hugunin, and then was changed over to NumPy by Travis Oliphant. Over the years, more contributors are going to help develop the NumPy over the years, and it is open sourced which will allow us to really see what can work with it over time.

The Python programming language was able to do a lot of different things over time. With that said, in the beginning, it wasn't designed to do any computing of numbers. However, because it is so easy to work with and has enough power that goes with it, it was able to attract the attention of the scientific and engineering community early on, and this group was interested in learning how they could use Python for their own needs.

Because of this, in 1995 a special interest group, which went under the name of matrix-sig, was founded and their aim was to make a computing package that can work with arrays and handle some of the numerical computing that scientists and engineers could use. Among the members of this group was the well-known Python maintainer and designer named Guido van

Rossum, who then implemented some of these extensions of the Python syntax (in particular, it is going to use the indexing syntax, to make the array computing a bit easier overall.

One of the goals that came with this is that it was meant to replace Numerically, and hopefully, it would come in as being a bit more flexible compared to the older version. Like Numeric, it is now deprecated. Numarray, a version of NumPy, had a faster operation for some of the larger arrays, but on some of the smaller ones, it would be slower.

Numeric and Numarray were in competition for some time, but then in 2005, the developer known as Travis Oliphant wanted to be able to make both of these, and take the benefits of each and turn them into one program or one library that would work the best for everyone. The new project became a part of the larger SciPy programming methods that were going on at the same time. However, to make sure that programmers were not needing to install the large SciPy package in order to get the NumPy program out of it, this was separated out. You can choose to either just get the SciPy library if you feel like you need more than one library from it, but if you are just interested in working with NumPy, you will be able to do this on its own as well.

So, to make this a bit easier to look at, let's explore a bit about what the NumPy library is all about, and why this is going to be such an important library to work with. Some of the things that make up the NumPy library to help us see why it is so important to include:

NumPy is going to be a numerical library available through Python that is open source so anyone is able to use it and see how it will work for them.

You will find that this library is going to contain a multi-dimensional matrix and array data structure.

You will be able to do quite a few operations that are mathematical on arrays. Some of the options that you are able to use with this one will include transformation, algebraic, and mathematical functions.

It is possible to work with random number generators as well.

NumPy is known as a wrapper that is going to be a library that can be implemented in C.

Pandas objects will rely on the objects of NumPy. Basically, these Pandas are going to extend the NumPy.

If you plan to work with the NumPy library, then this is a sign that you want to be able to write some of your own mathematical equations with the library. This makes it easier for you to really do some of the algebraic equations and other mathematical things that are a bit harder to work with if you just use the regular Python library. Not everyone is going to want to work with this option, but for some programmers it is necessary. The good news with this one is that you will be able to download just the NumPy library if you choose, making it easier to work with this library, without a lot of bloat and other objects and features that you do not need.

MATPLOTLIB

Another kind of library that you may choose to work with is going to be the Matplotlib. This one is a bit different than the library that we talked about before, and you will have to determine if this is a library that you will want to use along with the NumPy library from above, or if you will want to use this on its own. Not all programs are going to need this library, but it is still a good one to know about because, depending on the kinds of programs that you decide to write, you may need to bring this into the mix at some point.

Matplotlib is going to be one of the plotting libraries for the Python programming language. The neat thing is that this is a kind of extension that comes with NumPy, so if you do use that previous library, it is likely that you will need to bring in the Matplotlib as well. This extension is going to help you do some more numerical mathematics as well, but it is going to focus a bit more about the graphs and charts that you will want to work with that are based on the numbers that you have.

Matplotlib is going to be able to provide your program with an object-oriented API to embed plots into the application with a variety of different toolkits based on what you would like to use. This one is going to resemble the MATLAB that you may have heard about in the past, though the use of this is going to be highly discouraged. If you plan to use SciPy, which we will talk about in a bit, you will need to use the Matplotlib as well.

To take a look at the history of this library, you will find that John D. Hunter was the original writer of this library and it currently has a very active development community. This is good news if you plan to use the library because it means that the library is going to be developed and used a lot in the future and that any updates are going to be made available to you as quickly as possible.

Since this is an open-sourced library that you are able to work with, it has been changed up in order to support a lot of different versions of Python that are popular today. As of the summer of 2017, this library is able to support Python 2.7 to Python 3.6. However, since so many people are working with Python 3 right now, it is believed that by 2020, the library is not going to be supported on Python 2 any longer.

To help us get a better understanding of this kind of library, we also need to take some time to compare the Matplotlib to the idea of MATLAB. Pyplot is going to be a module that is found in Matplotlib and it is going to provide the computer with a MATLAB-like interface. Matplotlib is going to be designed in a manner that you are able to use it with MATLAB if you would like, and this allows you to use Python. The main advantage is that this makes it free and open source. You can choose whether you want to work with this or not with your own coding.

As we mentioned a bit before, you will be able to use the Matplotlib in order to deal with graphics and charts when you are working with the Python language. You are able to use it for a lot of different things including Python scrips, the shell, web application servers, and some other graphical user interface toolkits based on what you would like to do.

The neat thing here is that you can work with a lot of different tools in order to extend out the functionality of matplotlib. Different companies and developers have worked with these, and they are often going to be separate downloads. There are a few that can be downloaded at the same time as the source code for matplotlib, but they may have some external dependencies. Some of the ones that you may want to consider working with will include:

Basemap: This is going to be a toolkit that can help you to plot maps. This can include things like political boundaries, coastlines, and map projections.

Cartopy: This is going to be a mapping library that is going to include a lot of different options including image transformation capabilities, line, and polygon capabilities to name a few.

Excel tools: This is going to be a library that is able to provide you with some utilities to exchange the data you have with Microsoft Excel.

Mplot3d: This is the part that you are going to want to use with any 3D plots you want to do.

Natgrid: This is going to be an interface to the natgrid library for irregular gridding of the spaced data.

There are a few different types of plots and graphs that you are going to be able to use when you download and use the library of Matplotlib from Python. Some of the different types of graphs and plots that you are able to work with when you are doing this kind of library include:

The bar graph: A bar graph is going to rely on bars to help us compare data that shows up between different categories. It is going to be a good option if you would like to take a look at the changes that occur over a period of time. and you are able to represent it going either vertically or horizontally. In addition, this one works in a manner that shows us that the longer the bar is, the greater the value associated with it.

The histogram: Histograms are going to be used to help us see the distribution of something. These are going to be the most helpful when we are looking at a list that is really long or we work with arrays.

Scatterplot: Another option that you can go with is known as the scatter plot. The scatter plot is going to be used when you would like to compare variables, especially when you want to know how much one variable is going to be affected by another variable in order to build up a relationship that shows up there. The data for the scatter plot is going to be displayed as a collection of points, and the value that you have for one of your variables will determine the position on the horizontal axis. Then the value of the other variable is going to tell us the position that shows up on the vertical axis as well.

Area plot: This one is going to be similar to a line plot, and you may hear them called as a stack plot. These plots are meant to help the programmer track changes that occur over time for two or more related groups that will make up one whole category.

Pie chart: There may be some times when you want to work with a pie chart, and this library will help you to get it done. The pie chart is going to be a circular graph that can be broken down into smaller segments based on the information that you have. it is going to look similar to a pie, and each slice is going to show us the categories that you are working with at the time.

These are just a few of the different graphs and charts that you will be able to work with when it comes to the matplotlib library. It is going to be an extension that comes with the NumPy library that we talked about before, and you may find that these are both going to work together well. In fact, once you are done doing some of the mathematical equations from before, you will be able to take that information and turn it into some of the charts that are found with matplotlib.

If you are planning on doing some work with numbers and charts, you will find that the regular library that comes with

Python is just not going to be able to do all of the work on its own. This just wasn't what it was designed to do in the first place. But if this is something that is important to you and you need to get that done with the help of Python, then adding in the NumPy and the Matplotlib libraries are the best options to make this happen.

SCIPY

The last two options that we spent some time looking at were meant to help us with mathematical equations and some of the charts and graphs that we may want to create if we are using the Python language. With that in mind, it is time to move on to a different library that can still prove to be really useful when you work on Python. This library is known as SciPy and it is going to be a good Python approved library that works more for technical and scientific computing.

When you take a look at the SciPy library, you will notice that there will be a ton of modules that are found inside. Some of the modules that are found in this library will include ODE solvers, image and signal processing, FFT< special functions, interpolation, integration, linear algebra, optimization, and many other modules that are going to make it easier to do tasks of engineering and science.

As you can imagine, there are a lot of different modules and more that are going to fit in with this idea, which is what makes the SciPy library a great one to work with. This library is going to build upon the NumPy array object, and it is going to be included in the same stack of NumPy as matplotlib. This should tell you that you are likely to use SciPy at some point if you are already working with the other two libraries as well.

SciPy is also going to be distributed using the BSD license, and it has a development that has been sponsored, as well as supported, by a community of developers who work to keep it nice and open for others to use. You will also find that this library is going to be supported by NumFOCUS, which is a community foundation that has the goal of supporting reproducible and accessible science, especially in Python.

When you decide to download the SciPy library or the package that goes with it, you will find that there are going to be a number of key functions and algorithms that are going to be included in this. This is done to help Python expand out some of its computing capabilities to work more in the scientific world. Some of the sub packages that are included with this library, if you choose to use them, will include options like:

Weave. This is a good tool to work with if you would like to write out C and C++ as Python multiline strings.

Stats: This is a function to deal with statistics.

Special: This is going to include any of the special functions that are included in this library.

Spatial: This is going to include a lot of the different machine learning algorithms that you will want to work with including distance functions, nearest neighbors, and KD-treas.

Sparse: This one is good for sparse matrix and some of the algorithms that are related to it.

Signal: This is going to be a signal processing tool.

Optimize: This is going to use some algorithms that are meant for optimization, including some that have to do with linear programming.

Ndimage: This one is going to be useful to the programmer who wants to work with various functions that are meant for multi-dimensional image processing.

Misc: This is going to include some miscellaneous utilities such as image writing or reading.

Linalg: This one is a good option to work with when you are trying to do some things with linear algebra routines.

Lib: This is a wrapper from Python that helps with some of the external libraries that you are trying to do.

Io: This is a good extension that you can use when it comes to data input and output.

Interpolate: This is a good option when it comes to interpolation tools.

Integrate: This is a good extension to use when it comes to numerical integration routines.

Fftpack: discrete Fourier transforms algorithms.

Clusters: This is another example of working with machine learning when you are doing the SciPy library. This is a good one that you can bring out when you want to do some of the machine learning algorithms like K-means, vector quantization, and hierarchical clustering.

Constants: And the final extension that we are going to take a look at is going to be the physical constants and conversion factors that you can work with.

Now, when you are working with some of the data structures that are used by this library, you will see that the most basic of this is going to be the multidimensional array that it is able to take from the module of NumPy. Since it is going to be associated back with NumPy, you will be able to use some of the random number generations, Fourier transforms, and even some functions that work with linear algebra. But the SciPy is able to take this a bit further because it is going to help with equivalent functions in a way that the NumPy library is not able to do.

You may also find that the NumPy library is going to be used in order to provide us with an efficient container of data that is multidimensional and is able to deal with data types that are arbitrary. The reason that this is so important is that it allows the NumPy library to work in a seamless manner to integrate with a lot of different databases, no matter what you are trying to work with.

In many cases, the older versions that you may have of SciPy would use Numeric as the point where it could get its array type. Of course, this has changed since Numeric is no longer using, and the NumPy array code is the one that the newer and more updated types of SciPy are going to be able to use.

There is a lot that you are going to be able to get when you use the SciPy library rather than some of the other options out there. It is a great way to expand out what you are able to do with the Python code, especially when it comes to numbers and using it for various scientific and engineering kinds of uses. There are also many extensions that come with this, which makes it the perfect addition to consider when you want to work with some types of machine learning, engineering, and even with some scientific options.

SCIKIT-LEARN

And the final library that we are going to take a look at is going to be the Scikit-learn library. This is going to be free software that you can use, and it has been designed to specifically help out with machine learning with the help of the Python language. So, if you are going to do some kind of project or coding that needs to work with machine learning, this is definitely one of the libraries that you need to take the time to download and learn how to use.

When we take a look at this library, you will find that it includes a ton of different options with it, especially when it comes to machine learning. You will be able to find a lot of clustering algorithms, regression algorithms, and classification algorithms. This is a lot of information, but some of the algorithms that you are the most likely to use with machine learning and find beneficial will include things like DBSCAN, k-means, gradient boosting, random forests, and support vector machines. These all come together to help you do a lot of the machine learning work that you want while relying on the Python code to make it easier to work.

This kind of library is also going to work so that you can add in the SciPy and the NumPy libraries that we talked about before. This way, if you need to bring in some formulas that are more numerical or more scientific, you will be able to integrate all of these in together as well. You may find, especially if your end goal is to write some codes that are more about machine learning than anything else, that downloading all three of these libraries is going to be the best option to help you get things done.

For the most part, the Scikit-Learn library is going to be written out in Python, which makes machine learning easier for a lot of people. There are going to be a few of the core algorithms though those have been written out with the Cython option in order to help achieve the performance that you are looking for. For example, you may see that the support vector machines are going to be implemented with the Cython wrapper attached to it.

As we have mentioned a bit in this section so far, the Scikit-Learn library is going to be based on the idea that many programmers are going to want to work with machine learning. This is a newer type of coding that has really taken off because it opens up the door to a lot of different types of programming that we may not be able to do with just Python on its own. This makes it highly adaptable and will ensure that we are able to make programs that keep up with the technology that is being offered now.

Let's look a bit at what machine learning is here. There is a lot that goes with this type of technology, and it is beyond the scope of this guidebook to talk about this in detail. But a little exploration will help us to get a better idea of what we are able to do when it comes to this library.

Machine learning is basically a type of programming that is going to teach the computer program how to make decisions and learn on its own. There are times when it is impossible for the coder to go through and figure out what all the answers will be based on their user. They just can't do it all because of the complexity of the program. And because of this, they are going to turn to some of the algorithms that are found in machine learning to make this work.

The best way to see how this works is to look at some examples of it. If you have ever used a search engine, then machine learning is something that is right at your fingertips. The program is able to look at your search query and pull up some of the answers and results that it thinks are the best. Over time, it starts to learn what kinds of results you like to get and will make better predictions.

Voice recognition software, like what we find on computers, or even on some of the different products like the Amazon Echo, are going to use this machine learning as well. The coder is not able to go through and guess what the user is going to say all the time or their speech patterns. So the device is programmed in order to learn from mistakes and get better at recognizing what the user is telling it.

These are just a few of the examples of what you will be able to do when it comes to the idea of machine learning. And the Scikit-Learn library is going to have some of the different algorithms that you need to use in order to make these things happen. Downloading it will be the best way to ensure that you are able to set yourself up for the best results with doing some of your own machine learning.

There are a lot of different parts that come with the Scikit-learn library, and since it is going to be attached to machine learning so much, there is going to be a lot of parts that we may not be able to explore as a beginner. With that said, we need to first take a look at the API that comes with this kind of library. The API of this library is designed to have a few different guiding principles in mind to help it work, including:

Consistency: All of the objects that are on this program need to be able to share a common interface. This interface is going to be drawn from a limited set of methods, but the documentation needs to be consistent between them.

Inspection: All of the values that are specified for the parameter are going to be exposed as attributes that are public.

Limited object hierarchy: Only the algorithms that are going to be represented by Python classes. The datasets are going to be represented in a standard format. And then the names of the parameters that you use will be found as a standard string in Python.

Composition: Many of the tasks that you try to use in machine learning are going to be used and expressed more as a sequence of the fundamental algorithms. The Scikit-Learn library is going to try and use this idea as often as it can.

Sensible defaults: When the models that you are working with need to have a user specify the parameters, the library is going to try to step in and define the default value that is the most appropriate to use here.

The idea with this one is that all of these principles are going to make sure that this particular library is as easy to use as possible, once you have the chance to understand some of the basic principles. Each of the algorithms for machine learning that is used in this library is going to then be implemented with the help of the Estimator API. The reason that this one is used is that it is able to provide a consistent interface for these algorithms, while offering room for all of the different applications of machine learning to be used.

This is a great thing because it is going to save you a lot of time. As you work with machine learning, you will notice that there are many different applications that work with machine learning. And if you had to change up the interfaces that you were able to do with each one all of the time, this would be a big hassle. This interface can handle many, if not all, of the machine learning algorithms that you are going to work with, which is really going to make a difference in the results that you get, and how easy it is to work with machine learning on the Python code.

All of these libraries are going to be great options to work with. They add in some new functionality to what you are able to do with Python, making it easier to work on some of the different types of programming that you want to do with Python, even if the original Python program isn't set up to do them. You may find that adding in a few of these libraries to your program and learning how to use the algorithms and more that come with them can add in a bit more functionality to the codes that you are writing and can make it easier for you to really get the results that you need out of some of your written programs.

CONCLUSION

Thank for making it through to the end of Learning Python, let's hope it was informative and able to provide you with all of the tools you need to achieve your goals whatever they may be.

The next step is to start working on some of the different codes and options that we have presented in this guidebook. You will find that there are a lot of different things that you are able to work on, and the options are just going to be limited based on the kind of programming that you want to do. This guidebook went over a lot of different parts of the Python code so that you are prepared and have a full understanding of how the Python code is going to work, and how you are able to write the codes that are found inside.

This guidebook is meant to be a great introduction to working with the Python language. There are a lot of parts that come in, and many times a beginner is going to look at is all and be worried that they don't understand how it works, or that they will never be able to code at all. But with some of the examples and exercises that we explored in this guidebook, you will find that even some of the more complex parts of the code are going to be easier to handle, and you will be able to use those as ways to really write some of your own code along the way.

When you are ready to learn a bit more about the Python language and how you can use some of the aspects of this language to write your own codes, make sure to check out this guidebook to learn exactly how to get it done!

PYTHON MACHINE LEARNING

Discover the Essentials of Machine Learning, Data Analysis, Data Science, Data Mining and Artificial Intelligence using Python Code with Python Tricks

INTRODUCTION

Congratulations on purchasing *Python Machine Learning: Discover the essentials of machine learning, data analysis, data science, data mining and artificial intelligence using Python Code with Python tricks* and thank you for doing so.

The following chapters will discuss the core concepts of "Machine Learning" models that are being developed and advanced using Python programming language. This book will provide you overarching guidance on how you can use Python to develop machine learning models using Scikit-Learn and TensorFlow machine learning libraries. You will start this book by gaining a solid understanding of the basics of machine learning technology and types of machine learning models. It is important to master the concepts of machine learning technology and learn how researchers are breaking the boundaries of data science to mimic human intelligence in machines using various learning algorithms. The power of machine learning technology has already started to manifest in our environment and in our everyday objects.

The chapter 2 titled "Machine Learning Algorithms", you will learn the nuances of "12 of the most popular machine learning algorithms", in a very easy to understand language that requires no background in Python coding language and indeed might spike your interest in this field of research. You will learn about the foundational machine learning algorithms namely, supervised, unsupervised and reinforcement machine learning algorithms that serve as the skeleton of hundreds of machine learning algorithms being developed every day.

The chapter 3, titled "Basics of Data Science technologies", will provide you a clear and concise overview of various Data Science technologies that are shaping our present and will dictate our technological future, as experiences through the Fourth Industrial revolution. Data science is an umbrella term used for the cutting-edge technologies of today such as "big data or big data analytics", "data mining technology", "machine learning technology" and even "artificial intelligence technology".

In chapter 4, titled "Machine Learning Library "Scikit-Learn" 101", we deep dive into the functioning of Scikit-Learn library along with the pre-requisites required to develop machine learning model using Scikit-Learn library. A detailed walkthrough with an open-source database using illustrations and actual Python code that you can try hands-on by following the instructions in this book. There is no better way to learn than to get your hands dirty and get real experience of the task. There is also guidance provided on resolving nonlinear issues with "k-nearest neighbor" and "kernel trick algorithms" in this book.

You will learn the entire process of creating of Neural Network models on TensorFlow machine learning platform, using open source data set for example, along with the actual Python code used for the development, in chapter 5, titled "Neural Network training with TensorFlow". Neural Networks are characterized by a "single neuron-like entity of the machine that is capable of learning the expected output for a given input from training data sets". TensorFlow is built on Python and touted as a simple and flexible architecture that supports the development of machine learning ideas from "concept to code to state-of-the-art models and publication" in a short time.

In the last chapter of the book, titled "Data pre-processing and Creation of training data set", you will learn all about the most time consuming and critical aspect of developing a machine learning model i.e. Data pre-processing and splitting the processed data set into training and testing subsets. Finally, as a bonus, you will learn some Python tips and tricks to take your machine learning programming game to the next level. So, breathe in, breathe out, and let's begin!

There are plenty of books on this subject on the market, thanks again for choosing this one! Every effort was made to ensure it is full of as much useful information as possible, please enjoy!

CHAPTER 1: FUNDAMENTALS OF MACHINE LEARNING

The concept of Artificial Intelligence technology stems from the idea that machines are capable of human-like intelligence and can mimic human thought processing and learning capabilities, to adapt to new inputs and perform tasks without requiring human assistance. Machine learning is integral to the concept of artificial intelligence. Machine learning technology (ML) is referred to the concept of Artificial Intelligence technology that focuses primarily on the engineered capability of machines to explicitly learn and self-train, by identifying data patterns to improve upon the underlying algorithm and make independent decisions with no human intervention". In 1959, pioneering computer gaming and artificial intelligence expert, Arthur Samuel, coined the term "machine learning" during his tenure at IBM.

Machine learning hypothesizes that modern-day computers can be trained using targeted training data sets, that can be easily customized to develop desired functionalities. Machine learning is driven by the pattern recognition technique wherein the machine records and revisits past interactions and results, that are deemed in alignment with its current situation. Given the fact that machines are required to process the endless amount of data, with new data always pouring in, they must be equipped to adapt to the new data without needing to be programmed by a human, which speaks to the iterative aspect of ML.

Now the topic of machine learning is so "hot" that the academia, business world and the scientific community have their take on its definition. Here are some of the widely accepted definitions from select highly reputed sources:

- "Machine learning is the science of getting computers to act without being explicitly programmed." – Stanford University

- "The field of Machine Learning seeks to answer the question, how can we build computer systems that automatically improve with experience, and what are the fundamental laws that govern all learning processes?" – Carnegie Mellon University

- "Machine learning algorithms can figure out how to perform important tasks by generalizing from examples." – University of Washington

- "Machine Learning at its most basic is the practice of using algorithms to parse data, learn from it, and then decide or prediction about something in the world." – Nvidia

- "Machine learning is based on algorithms that can learn from data without relying on rules-based programming." – McKinsey.

BASIC CONCEPTS OF MACHINE LEARNING

The biggest draw of machine learning is the engineered capability of the system to learn programs from the data automatically instead of manually constructing the program for the machine. Over the last decade, the use of machine learning algorithms expanded from computer science to the industrial world. Machine learning algorithms are capable of generalizing tasks to execute them iteratively. The process of developing specific programs for specific tasks costs a lot of time and money, but occasionally it's just impossible to achieve. On the other hand, ML programming is often feasible and tends to be much more cost-effective. The use of machine learning in tackling ambitious issues of widespread importance such as global warming and depleting underground water levels is promising with a massive collection of relevant data.

"A breakthrough in machine learning would be worth ten Microsoft."

– Bill Gates

Many types of machine learning exist today but the concept of machine learning largely boils down to three components "representation", "evaluation" and "optimization". Here are some of the standard concepts that apply to all of them.

REPRESENTATION

Machine learning models are incapable of directly hearing, seeing or sensing input examples. Therefore, data representation is required to supply the model with a useful vantage point into the key qualities of the data. To be able to successfully train a machine learning model selection of key features that best represent the data is very important. "Representation" simply refers to the act of "representing" data points from a computer to a language that it understands using a set of classifiers. A classifier can be defined as "a system that inputs a vector of discrete and or continuous feature values and outputs a single discrete value called class". For a model to learn from the represented data the training data set or the "hypothesis space" must contain the desired classifier that you want the models to be trained on. Any classifiers that are external to the hypothesis space cannot be learned by the model.

The data features used to represent the input are very critical to the machine learning process. The data features are so important to the development of the desired machine learning model that can easily be the difference between successful and failed machine learning projects. A training data set containing multiple independent "features" that are well correlated with the "class" can make the machine learning much smoother. On the other hand, the class containing complex features may not be easy to learn from for the machine. This often requires the raw data to be processed so that desired features can be constructed from it, to be leveraged for the ML model. The process of deriving features from raw data tends to be the most time consuming and laborious part of the ML project. It is also considered the most creative and interesting part of the project where intuition and trial and error play just as important role as the technical requirements.

The process of ML is not a "one-shot process" of developing a training data set and executing it instead it is an iterative process that requires analysis of the post-run output, followed by modification of the training data set and then repeating the whole process all over again. Another reason for the extensive time and effort required to engineer the training data set is domain specificity. Training data set for an e-commerce platform to generate predictions based on consumer behavior analysis will be very different from the training data set required to develop a self-driving car. However, the actual machine learning process remains largely the same across industrial domains. No wonder, a lot of research is being done to automate the feature engineering process.

EVALUATION

Essentially the process of judging multiple hypothesis or models to choose one model over another is referred to as an evaluation. To be able to differentiate between useful classifiers from the vague ones an "evaluation function" is required. The evaluation function is also called as "objective", "utility" or "scoring" function. The machine learning algorithm has its internal evaluation function which tends to be different from the external evaluation function used by the researchers to optimize the classifier. Usually, the evaluation function is defined before the selection of the data representation tool, as the first step of the project. For example, the machine learning model for a self-driving car has the feature for identification of pedestrians in its vicinity at near-zero false negatives and a low false-positive as an evaluation function and the pre-existing condition that needs to be "represented" using applicable data features.

OPTIMIZATION

The process of searching the space of presented models to achieve better evaluations or highest-scoring classifier is called as "optimization". For algorithms with more than one optimum classifier, the selection of optimization technique is very critical in the determination of the classifier produced and to achieve a more efficient learning model. A variety of off-the-shelf optimizers are available in the market to kick start new machine learning models before eventually replacing them with custom-designed optimizers.

Representation	Evaluation	Optimization
Table 1. The three components of learning algorithms.		
Instances	Accuracy/Error rate	Combinatorial optimization
K-nearest neighbor	Precision and recall	Greedy search
Support vector machines	Squared error	Beam search
Hyperplanes	Likelihood	Branch-and-bound
Naive Bayes	Posterior probability	Continuous optimization
Logistic regression	Information gain	Unconstrained
Decision trees	K-L divergence	Gradient descent
Sets of rules	Cost/Utility	Conjugate gradient
Propositional rules	Margin	Quasi-Newton methods
Logic programs		Constrained
Neural networks		Linear programming
Graphical models		Quadratic programming
Bayesian networks		
Conditional random fields		

BASIC MACHINE LEARNING TERMINOLOGIES

Agent – In the context of reinforcement learning, an agent refers to "the entity that uses a policy to maximize expected return gained from transitioning between states of the environment".

Boosting – Boosting can be defined as "a machine learning technique that iteratively combines a set of simple and not very accurate classifiers (referred to as weak classifiers) into a classifier with high accuracy (a strong classifier) by up-weighting the examples that the model is currently misclassifying".

Candidate generation – The phase of selecting the "first set of recommendations" by a recommendation system is referred to as candidate generation. For example, a book library can offer 500,000 titles. This technique will produce a subset of few 100 books meeting the needs of a particular user and can be refined further to an even smaller set as needed.

Categorical Data – Data features boasting a "discrete set of possible values" is called as categorical data. For example, a "categorical feature" labeled car style can have an unconnected set of multiple possible values including sedan, coupe, SUV.

Checkpoint – Checkpoint can be defined as "The data that can capture the state of the variables of a learning model particular moment in time". With the use of checkpoints, training can be carried out across multiple sessions and model weights or scores can be exported.

Class – Class can be defined as "one of a set of listed target values for a given label". For example, a machine learning model designed to detect "spam" will have two classes, namely, "spam" and "not spam".

Classification model – The type of ML model used to "distinguish between two or more discrete classes of data" is referred to as a classification model. For example, a classification model for identification of dog breeds could assess whether the dog picture used as input is Labrador, Schnauzer, German Shepherd, Beagle and so on.

Collaborative filtering – The process of generating predictions for a particular user based on the shared interests of a group of similar users is called collaborative filtering.

Continuous feature – It is defined as a "floating-point feature with an infinite range of possible values".

Discrete feature – It is defined as a "rigid feature with a finite set of possible values".

Discriminator – "The system that determines whether the input examples are real or fake" is called discriminator.

Down-sampling – The process of Down-sampling refers to "the act of reducing the amount of information contained in a feature or using a disproportionately low percentage of over-represented class examples to train the learning model more efficiently".

Dynamic model – A learning model that is continuously receiving input data to be trained continuously is called dynamic model.

Ensemble – "The set of predictions generated by merging predictions of multiple models" is called ensemble.

Environment – The term 'environment' used in the context of reinforcement machine learning constitutes "the world that contains the agent and allows the agent to observe that world's state".

Episode – The term episode used in the context of reinforcement machine learning constitutes "every iterative attempt made by the agent to learn from its environment".

Feature – "An input data variable that is used in generating predictions" is called feature.

Feature engineering – Feature engineering can be defined as "the process of determining which features might be useful in training a model, and then converting raw data from log files and other sources into said features".

Feature extraction – Feature extraction can be defined as "the process of Retrieving intermediate feature representations calculated by an unsupervised or pre-trained model for use in another model as input".

Few-shot learning - Few-shot learning can be defined as "a machine learning approach, often used for object classification, designed to learn effective classifiers from only a small number of training examples".

Fine-tuning – The process of "performing a secondary optimization to adjust the parameters of an already trained model to fit a new problem" is called as fine-tuning. It is widely used to refit the weights of a "trained unsupervised model" to a "supervised model".

Generalization – "The ability of the machine learning model to make correct predictions on new, previously unseen data as opposed to the data used to train the model" is called generalization.

Inference – In the context of ML, an inference can be defined as "the process of making predictions by applying the trained model to unlabeled examples".

Label – In the context of machine learning (supervised), the "answer" or "result" part of an example is called label. A labeled data set can constitute single or multiple features and corresponding labels for every example. For example, in a house data set, the features could include the year built, number of bedrooms and bathrooms, while the label can be the "house's price".

Linear model – Linear model is defined as "a model that assigns one weight per feature to make predictions".

Loss – In the context of machine learning, loss refers to the "measure of how far are the predictions generated by the model from its label".

Matplotlib – It is "an open-source Python 2D plotting library which is used to visualize different aspects of machine learning".

Model – In the context of ML, a model can be defined as "the representation of what a machine learning system has learned from the training data".

NumPy – "An open-source math library that provides efficient array operations in Python".

One-shot learning – In the context of ML, one-shot learning refers to "a machine learning approach designed to learn effective classifiers from a single training example, often used for object classification".

Overfitting - In the context of machine learning, overfitting is referred to as "creation of a model that matches the training data so closely that the model fails to make correct predictions on new data".

Parameter – "A variable of a model that the machine learning system can train on its own" is called parameter.

Pipeline – In the context of ML, pipeline refers to "the infrastructure surrounding a machine learning algorithm and includes a collection of data, addition of the data to training data files, training one or more models, and exporting the models to production".

Random forest – In the context of machine learning, the concept of random forest pertains to "an ensemble approach for finding the decision tree that best fits the training data by developing multiple decision trees with a random selection of features".

Scaling - In the context of machine learning, scaling refers to "a common feature engineering practice to tame a feature's range of values to match the range of other features in the dataset".

Sequence model - A sequence model simply refers to a model with sequential dependency on data inputs to generate a future prediction.

Under-fitting - In the context of ML, under-fitting refers to "production of a ML model with poor predictive ability because the model hasn't captured the complexity of the training data".

Validation – "The process used to evaluate the quality of a machine learning model using the validation set, as part of the model training phase" is called as validation. The main goal of this process is to make sure that the performance of the ML model can be applied beyond the training set.

TYPES OF MACHINE LEARNING MODELS

Artificial Neural Networks

"Artificial Neural Networks" or (ANN) have been developed with inspiration from the structure of the human brain and utilizes numerous processing units like human neurons or nodes working as one. Each ANN has numerous concealed layers including an input and an output layer. These neurons are connected in a complex with one another by weighted links. A solitary neuron is capable of accepting input from various neurons. When a neuron gets activated, it casts a "weighted vote" to control the activation of the subsequent neuron that is collecting that input. An algorithm modifies these weights following the training data to optimize learning. A simple algorithm called "fire together, wire together" increases the weight between two connected neurons when the activation of either neuron leads to subsequent activation of the other neuron. "Concepts" are formed and distributed through the sub-network of shared neurons.

The most widely recognized ANN deal with the unidirectional progression of information and are called "Feed forward ANN". However, ANN can also be used for bidirectional and cyclic progression of information to gain state equilibrium. ANNs are less dependent on prior assumptions and able to learn from prior cases by modifying the connected weights. They can be utilized with either supervised or unsupervised learning. The use of supervised learning will generate correct ANN output for every input pattern. By varying the weights, the error between the target output and the output produced by ANN can be effectively minimized. For example, a type of "supervised learning algorithm" called "reinforced learning", informs the ANN whether the output it produced is correct or not instead of directly supplying the correct output. On the other hand, "unsupervised learning algorithm" is capable of providing a variety of input pattern to the ANN which is then processed by the ANN to self-explore the relationship between the provided input patterns and learn to categorize them accordingly. Artificial Neural Networks utilizing a combination of "supervised" and "unsupervised" learning are also available.

ANN is the choice of the learning model to address data-driven problems with unknown or difficult to comprehend algorithm or rules, credited to their defined data structure and non-linear computations. ANNs are capable of efficiently processing complex information and can easily withstand multi-variable data errors. Problems requiring a complete understanding of and insight into the actual process are not suitable for the ANN model, given its black box nature providing no view into the underlying process.

ANNs are widely used to resolve problems that require:

- "Pattern classification" by assigning input pattern to one of the pre-determined classes. For example, classification of land-based on satellite images.

- "Clustering", which is simply an unsupervised pattern classification model. For example, the prediction of the ecological status of water streams using defined input patterns.

- "Function approximation or regression", which is capable of creating a function out of the provided set of training patterns. For example, prediction of ozone concentration in the atmosphere, estimation of the amount of nitrate in groundwater and modeling water supply.

- "Prediction", which utilized prior data samples in a time series to estimate the output. For example, prediction of air and water quality.

- "Optimization", which is used to maximize or minimize a "cost function" subject to predefined constraints. For example, calibration of infiltration equations.

- "Retrieval by content", which is capable of recalling memory even if the input is incomplete or distorted. For example, using satellite images to produce water quality proxies.

- "Process control", which seeks to keep the velocity under changing data load close to constant by changing the throttle angle. For example, engine speed control.

Genetic Algorithms

As one can gather from the name, Genetic Algorithm (GA) mimics the nature's theory of selection by transferring the traits of the fitter solutions to the "offspring" and supplanting the less fit solutions. The Genetic Algorithm will keep evolving until a desired solution of the problem is achieved. Similar to human chromosomes, every potential solution is encoded as a "binary string" of traits and each arrangement of the progressive population are referred to as "generations". The original population set is produced randomly and all superseding generations are created through the process of selection and reproduction. A specific subset of the populace is then selectively bred to produce new chromosomes. The process of selection is driven by the fitness of the individual solutions including closeness to a perfect solution and deterministic examining. The closeness to a perfect selection is frequently carried out by the "roulette selection" method leading to the arbitrary selection of a parent with calculated probability based on its fitness. Then the deterministic examining allots a value to a subset of a selected organism.

Conventional propagation is achieved through genetic crossover, which produces the off-spring by trading chromosomes from two parents and inserting mutations in the chromosome to randomly modify some portion of the parent chromosome. The propagation doesn't happen as often as in the human world but allows the introduction of new genetic material in the gene pool. Mutation is considered less important than crossover in the advancement of the search but is deemed vital in the maintenance of genetic diversity, which is fundamental to continued evolution. In steady-state genetic algorithms, fewer fit members are superseded by the new generation, bringing about an increase in the average fitness of the model. The cycle of "reproduction and selection" is repeated until the completion criteria are met, for example, optimum fitness has been reached or all organisms are identical and evolution is not generating new results.

By focusing only on fitness examination and not accounting for other derivatives, genetic algorithms are considered highly robust computationally and capable of can smoothly balance load and efficacy. Another significant aspect of the genetic algorithm is its capability to indirectly sample a big volume of code sequences that have been tested. Unlike the stochastic search techniques which cannot search through noisy and multimodal relations, genetic algorithm can store a whole population of solutions instead of adjusting just a single solution. Some application examples of genetic algorithms include: "forecasting air quality, calibration of the water-quality models, estimation of soil bulk density and water management systems".

Decision trees - A machine learning decision tree can be defined as "a tree-like graphical representation of the decision-making process, by taking into consideration all the conditions or factors that can influence the decision and the consequences of those decisions". Decision trees are considered one of the simplest "supervised machine learning algorithms" and has three main elements: "branch nodes" representing conditions of the data set, "edges" representing ongoing decision process and "leaf nodes" representing the end of the decision. Decision trees make for an excellent predictive analysis technique with wide application in generating predictions for the values of "categorical" as well as "continuous" target variables. (Note – The very important concept of Decision Trees will be explored in details in the next chapter of this book)

Probabilistic Programming

"Probabilistic programming" is a high-level programming language that empowers formation of probability models, with the capability to extract values from distributions and condition these values into a program. The Probabilistic programming based learning systems are capable of making inferences from earlier knowledge, permitting decision making even in the face of uncertainty. To capture the knowledge of the target system "quantitative" and "probabilistic" terms are utilized. With adequate training, the model can be applied to explicit inquires to generate answers through a process called "inference".

With the use of probabilistic programming language, the probability model can also be solved automatically without any external assistance. It also supports uninterrupted access and reusability of machine learning model libraries and provides support for interactive modeling as well as formal verification. The abstraction layer within the probabilistic algorithm is paramount to nurture generic and efficient inferences because various Artificial Intelligence problems require the agent to process fragmented and distorted data set. Probabilistic algorithms are widely used to analyze large volumes of data to generate predictions and assist perception systems in the analysis of the underlying processes. Some examples of Probabilistic programming applications are: "medical imaging", "financial predictions", "machine perception" and "weather forecasting".

The most widely used probabilistic model is called "Bayesian network", which uses "Bayesian inference" to compute probability. The Bayesian network can generate inferences in two forms. The first one is the assessment of the joint probability of a specific assignment of values for every single variable in the network. While the second form is the assessment of the probability of a subset of variables that have been given assignments of an alternate subset of variables. The problems about reasoning, learning, planning, and perception of the system can be addressed with the application of the Bayesian networks. The "Bayesian inference algorithm" is utilized in the resolution of reasoning problems while the "expectation" and "maximization" algorithm can be used to address learning problems. The dynamic Bayesian networks allow for unfettered perception and decision networks which are widely used to solve planning issues.

MACHINE LEARNING IN PRACTICE

The complete process of machine learning is much more extensive than just the development and application of machine learning algorithms and can be divided into steps below:

1. Define the goals of the project taking into careful consideration all the prior knowledge and domain expertise available. Goals can easily become ambiguous

since there are always additional things you want to achieve than practically possible to implement.

2. The data pre-processing and cleaning must result in a high-quality data set. This is the most critical and time-consuming step of the whole project. The larger the volume of data, the more noise it brings to the training data set which must be eradicated before feeding to the learner system.

3. Selection of appropriate learning model to meet the requirements of your project. This process tends to be rather simple given the various types of data models available in the market.

4. Depending on the domain the machine learning model is applied to, the results may or may not require a clear understanding of the model by human experts as long as the model can successfully deliver desired results.

5. The final step is to consolidate and deploy the knowledge or information gathered from the model to be used on an industrial level.

6. The whole cycle from step 1 to 5 listed above is iteratively repeated until a result that can be used in practice is achieved.

IMPORTANCE OF MACHINE LEARNING

To get a sense of how significant machine learning is in our everyday lives, it is simpler to state what part of our cutting edge way of life has not been touched by it. Each aspect of human life is being impacted by the "smart machines" intended to expand human capacities and improve efficiencies. Artificial Intelligence and machine learning technology is the focal precept of the "Fourth Industrial Revolution", that could question our thoughts regarding being "human".

Here are a few reasons to help you understand the significance of machine learning in our daily lives:

- Automation of repetitive learning and revelation from data. Not at all like hardware-driven robotic automation that simply automates manual assignments, machine learning allows performance of high volume, computer-based tasks consistently and dependably.

- Machine learning algorithms are helping Artificial Intelligence to adapt to the evolving world by allowing the machine or system to learn, take note and improve upon its prior errors. Machine learning algorithm functions as a classifier or a predictor to acquire new skills and identify data pattern and structure. For example, machine learning algorithm has generated a system that can teach itself how to play chess and even how to generate product recommendations based on customer activity and behavior data. The beauty of this model is that it adapts with every new set of data.

- Machine learning has analyzed deeper and larger data set feasible with the use of neural networks containing multiple hidden layers. Think about it, a fraud detection system with numerous concealed layers would deem a work of fantasy just a couple of years ago. With the advent of big data and unlikely to envision computer powers, a whole new world is on the horizon. The data of the machines resemble the gas to the vehicle, the more data you can add to them, faster and more accurate results will get. Deep learning models flourish with an abundance of data because they gain straightforwardly from the data.

- The "deep neural networks" of the machine learning algorithms have resulted in unbelievable accuracy. For example, frequent and repeated use of smart tech like "Amazon Alexa" and "Google Search", results in increased accuracy derived from deep learning. These "deep neural networks" are also empowering our medical field. Image classification and object recognition are now capable of finding cancer on MRIs with similar accuracy as that of a highly trained radiologist.

- Artificial Intelligence is allowing for enhanced and improved use of big data analytics in conjunction with machine learning algorithms. Data has evolved as its currency and when algorithms are self-learning it can easily become "intellectual property". The raw data is similar to a gold mine in that the more and deeper you dig, the more "gold" or valuable insight you can dig out or extract. Application of machine learning algorithms to the data can enable you to find the correct solutions quicker and makes for an upper hand. Keep in mind the best information will consistently win, although everyone is utilizing comparative techniques.

CHAPTER 2: MACHINE LEARNING ALGORITHMS

By utilizing prior computations and underlying algorithms, machines are now capable of learning from and training on their own to generate high-quality, readily reproducible decisions and results. The notion of machine learning has been around for a long time now, but the latest advances in machine learning algorithms have made large data processing and analysis feasible for computers. This is achieved by applying sophisticated and complicated mathematical calculations using high speed and frequency automation. Today's advanced computing machines can analyze humongous information quantities quickly and deliver quicker and more precise outcomes. Companies using machine learning algorithms have increased flexibility to change the training data set to satisfy their company needs and train the machines accordingly. These tailored algorithms of machine learning enable companies to define potential hazards and possibilities for development. Typically, machine learning algorithms are used in cooperation with artificial intelligence technology and cognitive techniques to create computers extremely efficient and extremely effective in processing large quantities of information or big data and to generate extremely precise outcomes.

There are four fundamental types of machine learning algorithms available today.

SUPERVISED MACHINE LEARNING ALGORITHMS

Due to their ability to evaluate and apply the lessons learned from prior iterations and interactions to fresh input data set, the supervised learning algorithms are commonly used in predictive big data analysis. Based on the instructions given to effectively predict and forecast future occurrences, these algorithms can label all their ongoing runs. For instance, people can program the machine as "R" (Run), "N" (Negative) or "P" (Positive) to label its data points. The algorithm for machine learning will then label the input data as programmed and obtain data inputs with the right outputs. The algorithm will compare its own produced output to the "anticipated or correct" output, identifying future changes that can be created and fixing mistakes to make the model more precise and smarter. By using methods such as "regression," "prediction," "classification" and "ingredient boosting" to train the machine learning algorithms well, any new input data can be fed into the machine as a set of "target" data to orchestrate the learning program as desired. This "known training data set" jump-starts the analytical process followed by the learning algorithm to produce an "inferred feature" that can be used to generate forecasts and predictions based on output values for future occurrences. For instance, financial institutions and banks rely strongly on monitoring machine learning algorithms to detect credit card fraud and predict the probability of a prospective credit card client failing to make their credit payments on time.

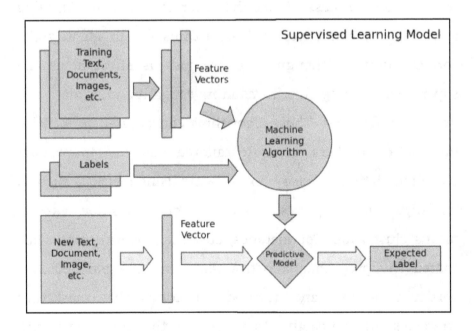

UNSUPERVISED MACHINE LEARNING ALGORITHMS

Companies often find themselves in a scenario where information sources are inaccessible that are needed to produce a labeled and classified training data set. Using unsupervised ML algorithms is perfect in these circumstances. Unsupervised ML algorithms are widely used to define how the machine can generate "inferred features" to elucidate a concealed construct from the stack of unlabeled and unclassified data collection. These algorithms can explore the data to define a structure within the data mass. Unlike the supervised machine learning algorithms, the unsupervised algorithms fail to identify the correct output, although they are just as effective as the supervised learning algorithms in investigating input data and drawing inferences. These algorithms can be used to identify information outliers, generate tailored and custom product recommendations, classify text subjects using methods such as "self-organizing maps," "singular value decomposition" and "k-means clustering." For instance, customer identification with shared shopping characteristics that can be segmented into particular groups and focused on comparable marketing strategies and campaigns. As a result, in the online marketing world, unsupervised learning algorithms are extremely popular.

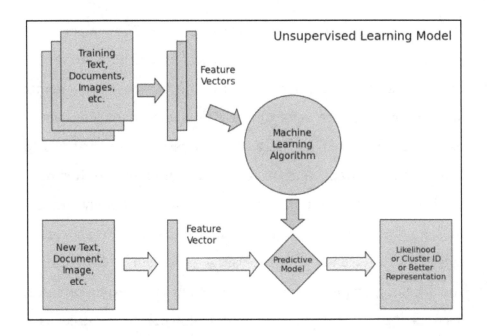

SEMI-SUPERVISED MACHINE LEARNING ALGORITHMS

Highly versatile, the "semi-supervised machine learning algorithms" are capable of using both labeled and unlabeled information set to learn from and train themselves. These algorithms are a "hybrid" of algorithms that are supervised and unsupervised. Typically, with a small volume of labeled data, the training data set is comprised of predominantly unlabeled data. The use of analytical methods including "forecast," "regression" and "classification" in conjunction with semi-supervised learning algorithms enable the machine to considerably enhance its learning precision and training capabilities. These algorithms are commonly used in instances where it is highly resource-intensive and less cost-effective for the business to generate labeled training data set from raw unlabeled data. Companies use semi-supervised learning algorithms on their systems to avoid incurring extra costs of staff and equipment. For instance, the implementation of "facial recognition" technology needs a huge amount of facial data distributed across various sources of input. The raw data pre-processing, processing, classification and labeling, acquired from sources such as internet cameras, needs a lot of resources and hours of work to be used as a training data set.

REINFORCEMENT MACHINE LEARNING ALGORITHMS

The "reinforcement machine learning algorithms" are much more distinctive in that they learn from the environment. These algorithms conduct activities and record the outcomes of each action diligently, which would have been either a failure resulting in mistake or reward for good performance. The two primary features that differentiate the reinforcement learning algorithms are the research method of "trial and error" and feedback loop of "delayed reward." Using a range of calculations, the computer constantly analyzes input data and sends a reinforcement signal for each right or anticipated output to ultimately optimize the final result. The algorithm develops a straightforward action gaining feedback loop to evaluate, record and learn which actions have been effective and in a shorter time have resulted in correct or expected output. The use of these algorithms allows the system to automatically determine optimal behaviors and maximize its efficiency within the constraints of a particular context. The reinforcement machine learning algorithms are therefore strongly used in gaming, robotics engineering, and navigation systems.

The machine learning algorithms have proliferated to hundreds and thousands and counting. Here are some of the most widely used algorithms:

1. Regression

The methods of "regression" fall under the supervised machine learning category. They assist in predicting or describing a specific numeric value based on the set of preceding data, such as anticipating a property's price based on preceding price data for comparable properties. Regression methods range from simple (such as "linear regression") to complex (such as "regular linear regression", "polynomial regression", "decision trees", "random forest regression" and "neural networks", among others).

The easiest technique of all is "linear regression", where the "mathematical equation of the line ($y = m * x + b$) is used to model a data set". A "linear regression" model can be trained with multiple "data pairs (x, y)" by calculating a line's position and slope that can reduce the overall distance between data points and the line. In other words, for a line that generates the best approximation for the data observations, the calculation of the "slope (m)" and "y-intercept (b)" is used.

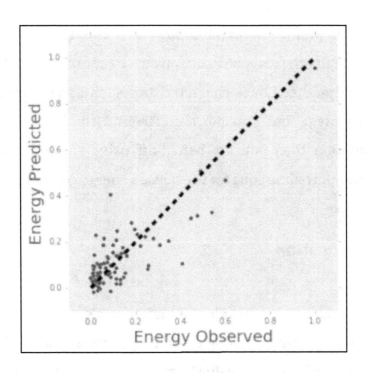

For example, using "linear regression" technique to generate predictions for the energy consumption (in kWh) of houses by collecting the age of the house, some bedrooms, square footage area, and several installed electronic equipment. Now, we have more than one input (year built, square footage) it is possible to use "linear multi-variable regression". The underlying process is the same as "one-to-one linear regression", however, the "line" created was based on the number of variables in multi-dimensional space.

The above plot demonstrates how well this model of linear regression fits the real construction energy consumption. In case you could gather house characteristics such as year built and square footage, but you don't understand the house's energy consumption then you are better off using the fitted line to generate approximations for the house's energy consumption.

2. Classification

The method of "classification" is another class of "supervised machine learning", which can generate predictions or explanations for a "class value". For example, this method can be used to predict the if of an online customer will purchase a particular product. The result generated will be reported as a yes or no response i.e. "buyer" or "not a buyer". But techniques of classification are not restricted to two classes. A classification technique, for instance, could assist to evaluate whether a specified picture includes a sedan or a SUV. The output will be three different values in this case: 1) the picture contains a sedan, 2) the picture contains a SUV, or 3) the picture does not contain either a sedan or a SUV.

"Logistic regression" is considered the easiest classification algorithm, though the term comes across as a "regression" technique that is far from reality. "Logistic regression" generates estimations for the likelihood of an event taking place based on single or multiple input values. For example, to generate estimation for the likelihood of a student being accepted to a specific university, a "logistic regression" will use the standardized testing scores and university testing score for a student as inputs. The generated prediction is a probability, ranging between '0' and '1', where 1 is full assurance. For the student, if the estimated likelihood is greater than 0.5, then the prediction would be that they will be accepted. If the projected probability is less than 0.5, the prediction would be that they will be denied admission.

The following graph shows the ratings of past learners as well as whether they have been accepted. Logistic regression enables creation of a line that can represent the "decision boundary".

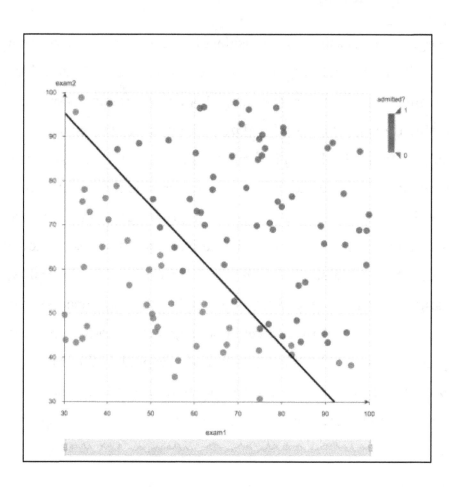

3. Clustering

We enter the category of unsupervised machine learning, with "clustering methods" because its objective is to "group or cluster observations with comparable features". Clustering methods do not use output data to train but allow the output to be defined by the algorithm. Only data visualizations can be used in clustering techniques to check the solution's quality.

"K-Means clustering", where 'K' is used to represent the number of "clusters" that the customer elects to generate and is the most common clustering method. (Note that different methods for selecting K value, such as the "elbow technique", are available.)

Steps used by K-Means clustering to process the data points:

1. The data centers are selected randomly by 'K'.

2. Assigns each data point to the nearest centers that have been randomly generated.

3. Re-calculates each cluster's center.

4. If centers do not change (or have minor change), the process will be completed.

Otherwise, we'll go back to step 2. (Set a maximum amount of iterations in advance to avoid getting stuck in an infinite loop, if the center of the cluster continues to alter.)

The following plot applies "K-Means" to a building data set. Each column in the plot shows each building's efficiency. The four measurements relate to air conditioning, heating, installed electronic appliances (refrigerators, TV) and cooking gas. For simplicity of interpretation of the results, 'K' can be set to value '2' for clustering, wherein one cluster will be selected as an efficient building group and the other cluster as an inefficient building group. You see the place of the structures on the left as well as a couple of the building characteristics used as inputs on the right: installed electronic appliances and heating.

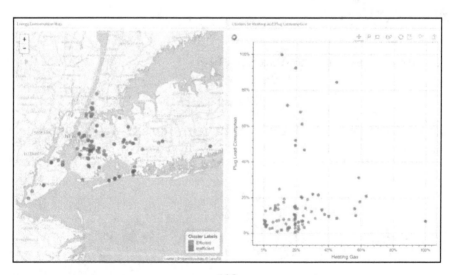

4. Dimension Reduction

As the name indicates, to extract the least significant information (sometimes redundant columns) from a data set, we use "dimensionality reduction". In practice, data sets tend to contain hundreds or even thousands of rows (also known as characteristics), which makes it essential to reduce the total number of rows. For example, pictures may contain thousands of pixels, all those pixels are not important for the analysis. Or a large number of measurements or experiments can be applied to every single chip while testing microchips within the manufacturing process, the majority of which produce redundant data. In such scenarios, "dimensionality reduction" algorithms are leveraged to manage the data set.

Principal Component Analysis

"Principal Component Analysis" or (PCA) is the most common "dimension reduction technique", which decreases the size of the "feature space" by discovering new vectors that are capable of maximizing the linear variety of the data. When the linear correlations of the data are powerful, PCA can dramatically decrease the data dimension without losing too much information. PCA is one of the fundamental algorithms of machine learning. It enables you to decrease the data dimension, losing as little information as possible. It is used in many fields such as object recognition, vision of computers, compression of information, etc. The calculation of the main parts is limited to the calculation of the initial data's vectors and covariance matrix values or of the data matrix's unique decomposition. Through one we can convey several indications, merge, so to speak, and operate with a simpler model already. Of course, most probably, data loss will not be avoided, but the PCA technique will assist us to minimize any losses.

t-Stochastic Neighbor Embedding (t-SNE)

Another common technique is "t-Stochastic Neighbor Embedding (t-SNE)", which results in a decrease of non-linear dimensionality. This technique is primarily used for data visualization, with potential use for machine learning functions such as space reduction and clustering.

The next plot demonstrates "MNIST database" analysis of handwritten digits. "MNIST" includes a large number of digit pictures from 0 to 9, used by scientists to test "clustering" and "classification" algorithms. Individual row of the data set represents "vectorized version" of the original picture (size 28x28 = 784 pixels) and a label (0, 1, 2 and so on) for each picture. Note that the dimensionality is therefore reduced from 784 pixels to 2-D in the plot below. Two-dimensional projecting enables visualization of the initial high-dimensional data set.

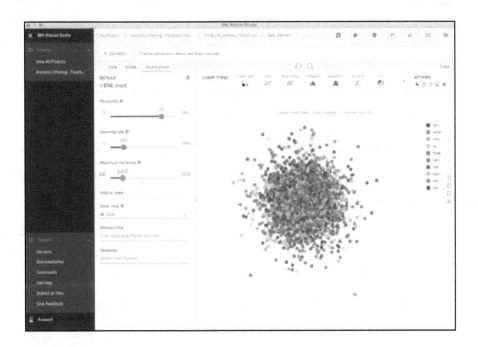

5. Ensemble Methods

Think that you have chosen to construct a car because you are not pleased with the variety of cars available in the market and online. You may start by discovering the best option for every component that you need. The resulting car will outshine all the other alternatives with the assembly of all these excellent components.

"Ensemble methods" use the same concept of mixing several predictive models (controlled machine learning) to obtain results of greater quality than any of the models can generate on their own. The "Random Forest" algorithms, for instance, is an "ensemble method" that collates various trained "Decision Trees" with different data set samples. Consequently, the quality of predictions generated by "Random Forest" method is better than the quality of the estimated predictions generated by only one "Decision Tree".

Think of "ensemble methods" as an approach for reducing a single machine learning model's variance and bias. This is essential because, under certain circumstances, any specified model may be accurate but completely incorrect under other circumstances. The relative accuracy could be overturned with another model. The quality of the predictions is balanced by merging the two models.

6. Transfer Learning

Imagine you are a data scientist focusing on the clothing industry. You have been training a high-quality learning model for months to be able to classify pictures of "women's tops" as tops, tank tops, and blouses. You have been tasked to create a comparable model for classification of pants pictures such as jeans, trousers, and chinos. With the use of "Transfer Learning" method, the understanding incorporated into the first model be seamlessly transferred and applied to the second model.

Transfer Learning pertains to the re-use and adaptation of a portion of a previously trained neural network to a fresh but comparable assignment. Specifically, once a neural network has been successfully trained for a particular task, a proportion of the trained layers can be easily transferred and combined with new layers which are then trained on pertinent data for the new task. This new "neural network" can learn and adapt rapidly to the new assignment by incorporating a few layers.

The primary benefit of transferring learning is decreasing in the volume of data required to train the neural network resulting in cost savings for development of "deep learning algorithms". Not to forget how hard it can be to even procure a sufficient amount of labeled data to train the model.

Suppose in this example, you are using a neural network with 20 hidden layers for the "women's top" model. You understand after running a few tests that 16 of the women's top model layers can be transferred and combined them with a new set of data to train on pants pictures. Therefore, the new pants model will have 17 concealed layers. The input and output of both the tasks are distinct, but the reusable layers are capable of summarizing the data appropriate to both, e.g. clothing, zippers, and shape of the garment.

Transfer learning is getting increasingly popular, so much so that for basic "deep learning tasks" such as picture and text classification, a variety of high quality pre-trained models are already available in the market.

7. Natural Language Processing

A majority of the knowledge and information of our world is in some type of human language. Once deemed as impossible to achieve, today computers are capable of reading large volumes of books and blogs within minutes. Although, computers are still unable to fully comprehend "human text", but they can be trained to perform specific tasks. Mobile devices, for instance, can be trained to auto-complete text messages or fix spelling mistakes. Machines have been trained enough to hold straightforward conversations like humans.

"Natural Language Processing" (NLP) is not exactly a method of ML, instead it is a commonly used technique to produce texts for machine learning. Consider a multitude of formats of tons of text files (words, internet blogs, etc). Most of these text files are usually flooded with typing errors, grammatically incorrect characters and phrases that need to be filtered out. The most popular text processing model available in the market today is "NLTK (Natural Language ToolKit)", developed by "Stanford University" researchers.

The easiest approach to map texts into numerical representations concern calculation of the frequency of each word contained in every text document. For example, an integer matrix where individual rows represent one text document and every column a single word. This word frequency representation matrix is frequently referred to as the "Term Frequency Matrix" (TFM). From there, individual matrix entries can be separated by weight of how essential every single term is within the whole stack of papers. This form of matrix representation of a text document is called "Term Frequency Inverse Document Frequency" (TFIDF), which usually yields better performance for machine learning tasks.

8. Word Embedding

"Term Frequency Matrix" and "Term Frequency Inverse Document Frequency" are numerical representations of text papers which only take into account frequency and weighted frequencies to represent text files. On the other hand, "Word Embedding" in a document is capable of capturing the actual context of a word. Embedding can quantify the similarity between phrases within the context of the word, which subsequently allows the execution of arithmetic operations with words.

"Word2Vec" is a neural network-based technique that can map phrases to a numerical vector in a corpus. These vectors are then used to discover synonyms, do arithmetic with words or phrases, or to represent text files. Let's suppose, for instance, a large enough body of text files was used to estimate word embedding. Suppose the words "king, queen, man, and female" are found in the corpus and vector ("word") is the number vector representing the word "word". We can conduct an arithmetic procedure with numbers to estimate vector('woman'):

vector('king')   +   vector('woman') — vector('man')   ~ vector('queen')

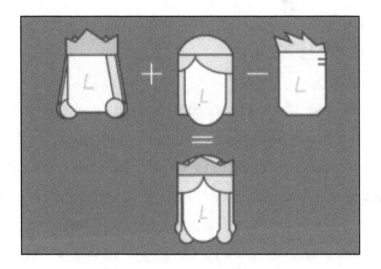

Word depictions enable similarities to be found between phrases by calculating the "cosine similarity" between the vector representation of the two words. The "cosine similarity" gives a measure of the angle between two vectors.

We use machine learning techniques to calculate word embedding, but this is often a preliminary step in implementing a machine learning algorithm on top of the word embedding method. For example, the "Twitter" user database containing a large volume of "tweets" can be leveraged to understand which of these customers purchased a house recently. We can merge "Word2Vec" with logistic regression to generate predictions on the likelihood of a new "Twitter" user purchasing a home.

9. Decision Trees

To refresh your memory; a machine learning decision tree can be defined as "a tree-like graphical representation of the decision-making process, by taking into consideration all the conditions or factors that can influence the decision and the consequences of those decisions". Decision trees are considered one of the simplest "supervised machine learning algorithms", with three main elements: "branch nodes" representing conditions of the data set, "edges" representing ongoing decision process and "leaf nodes" representing the end of the decision.

The two types of decision trees are: "Classification tree" that is used to classify Data based on the existing data available in the system; "Regression tree" which is used to make predictions for future events based on the existing data in the system. Both of these trees are heavily used in machine learning algorithms. A widely used terminology for decision trees is "Classification and Regression trees" or "CART".

Let's look at how you can build a simple decision tree based on a real-life example.

Step 1: Identify what decision needs to be made, which will serve as a "root node" for the decision tree. For this example, a decision needs to be made on "What would you like to do over the weekend?". Unlike real trees, the decision tree has its roots on top instead of the bottom.

Step 2: Identify conditions or influencing factors for your decision which will serve as "branch nodes" for the decision tree. For this example, conditions could include "would you like to spend the weekend alone or with your friends?" and "how is the weather going to be?".

Step 3: As you answer the conditional questions, you may run into additional conditions that you might have ignored. You will now continue to your final decision by processing all the conditional questions individually, these bifurcations will serve as "edges" of your decision tree.

Step 4: Once you have processed all of the permutations and combinations and eventually made your final decision, that final decision will serve as the "leaf node" of your decision tree. Unlike "branch nodes", there are no further bifurcations possible from a "leaf node".

Here is the graphical representation of your decision for the example above.

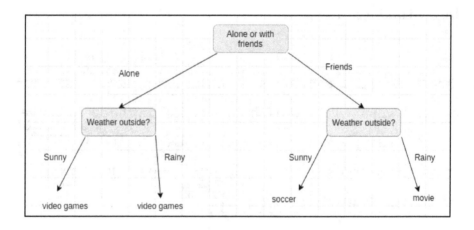

As you would expect from a decision tree, you have obtained a "model representing a set of sequential and hierarchical decisions that ultimately lead to some final decision". This example is at a very high-level to help you develop an understanding of the concept of decision trees. The data science and machine learning decision trees are much more complicated and bigger with hundreds and thousands of branch nodes and edges.

The best tool on the market to visualize and understand decision trees is "Scikit-Learn". Machine learning decisions tree models can be developed using two steps: "Induction" and "Pruning".

Induction

In this step, the decision trees are developed by selecting and modeling all of the sequential and hierarchical decision boundaries based on existing data set. For your ease of understanding, here are 4 high-level steps required to develop the tree:

1. Gather, classify and label the training data set with "feature variables" and "classification or regression output".

2. Identify the best and most cost-effective feature within the training data set that will be used as the point for bifurcating the data.

3. Based on the possible values of the selected "best feature", create subsets of data by bifurcating the data set. These bifurcations will define the "branch nodes" of the decision tree, wherein each node serves as a point of bifurcation based on specific features from the data set.

4. Iteratively develop new tree nodes with the use of data subsets gathered from step 3. These bifurcations will continue until an optimal point is reached, where maximum accuracy is achieved while minimizing the number of bifurcations or nodes.

Pruning

The inherent purpose of decision trees is to support training and self-learning of the system, which often requires overloading of all possible conditions and influencing factors that might affect the final result. To overcome the challenge of setting the correct output for least number of instances per node, developers make a "safe bet" by settling for that "least number" as rather small. This results in a high number of bifurcations on necessary, making for a very complex and large decision tree. This is where "tree pruning" comes into the picture. The verb "prune" literally means "to reduce especially by eliminating superfluous matter". This is the same kind of concept taken from real-life tree pruning and applied to the data science and machine learning decision tree pruning process.

The process of pruning effectively reduces the overall complexity of the decision tree by "transforming and compressing strict and rigid decision boundaries into generalized and smooth boundaries". The number of bifurcations of the decision trees determines the overall complexity of the tree. The easiest and widely used pruning method is reviewing individual branch nodes and evaluating the effect of its removal on the cost function of the decision tree. If the cost function has little to no effect of the removal, then the branch node under review can be easily removed or "pruned".

10. Apriori machine learning algorithm

"Apriori algorithm" is another unsupervised ML algorithm that can produce rules of the association from a specified set of data. "Association rule" simply means if an item X exists then the item Y has a predefined probability of existence. Most rules of association are produced in the format of "IF-THEN" statements. For instance, "IF" someone purchases an iPhone, "THEN" they have most likely purchased an iPhone case as well. The Apriori algorithm can draw these findings by initially observing the number of individuals who purchased an iPhone case while making an iPhone purchase and generating a ratio obtained by dividing the number individuals who bought a new iPhone (1000) with individuals who also bought an iPhone case (800) with their new iPhones.

The fundamental principles of Apriori ML Algorithm are:

- If a set of events have high frequency of occurrence, then all subsets of that event set will also have high frequency of occurrence.

- If a set of events occur occasionally, then all supersets of the event set of will occur occasionally as well.

Apriori algorithm has wide applicability in the following areas.

"Detecting Adverse Drug Reactions"

"Apriori algorithm" is used to analyze healthcare data such as the drugs administered to the patient, characteristics of each patient, harmful side effects experienced by the patient, the original diagnosis, among others. This analysis generates rules of association that provide insight into the character of the patient and the administered drug that potentially contributed to adverse side effects of the drug.

"Market Basket Analysis"

Some of the leading online e-commerce businesses including "Amazon", use Apriori algorithm to gather insights on products that have high likelihood of being bought together and products that can have an upsell with product promotions and discount offers. For instance, Apriori could be used by a retailer to generate prediction such as customers purchasing sugar and flour have high likelihood of purchasing eggs to bake cookies and cakes.

"Auto-Complete Applications"

The highly cherished auto-complete feature on "Google" is another common Apriori application. When the user starts typing in their keywords for a search, the search engine searches its database, for other related phrases that are usually typed in after a particular word.

11. Support vector machine learning algorithm

"Support Vector Machine" or (SVM) is a type of "supervised ML algorithm", used for "classification" or "regression", where the data set trains SVM on "classes" to be able to classify new inputs. This algorithm operates by classifying the data into various "classes" by discovering a line (hyper-plane) that divides the collection of training data into "classes". Due to availability of various linear hyper-planes, this algorithm attempts to maximize the distance between the different "classes" involved, which is called as "margin maximization". By identifying the line that maximizes the class distance, the likelihood of generalizing apparent to unseen data can be improved.

SVM's can be categorized into two as follows:

- "Linear SVM's" – The training data or classifiers can be divided by a hyper-plane.

- "Non-Linear SVM's" – Unlike linear SVMs, in "non-linear SVM's" the possibility to separate the training data with a hyper-plane is non-existent. For example, the Face Detection training data consists of a group of facial images and another group of non-facial images. The training data is so complicated under such circumstances, that it is difficult to obtain a feature representation of every single vector. It is extremely complex to separate the facial data set linearly from the non-facial data set.

SVM is widely used by different economic organizations for stock market forecasting. For example, SVM is leveraged to compare relative stock performances of various stocks in the same industrial sector. The classifications generated by SVM, aids in the investment-related decision-making process.

The Kernel Trick

The data collected in the real world is randomly distributed and making it too difficult to separate different classes linearly. However, if we can potentially figure out a way to map the data from 2-dimensional space to 3-dimensional space, as shown in the picture below, we will be able to discover a decision surface that separates distinct classes.

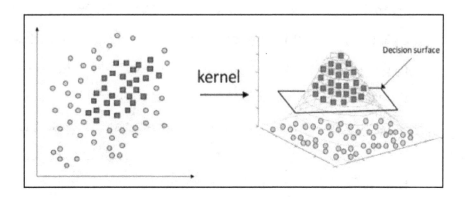

One approach to transforming data like this is mapping all data points to a higher dimension (in this case, 3 dimensions), finding the limit, and making the classification. That works for a limited number of dimensions but computations within given space become increasingly costly when there are a lot of dimensions to deal with. And so the kernel trick comes to the rescue!

The "kernel trick" enables us to function in the original feature space without needing to calculate the data coordinates in a higher-dimensional space. For example, the equation in the picture below has a couple of 3-D data points as 'x' and 'y'.

$$\mathbf{x} = (x_1, x_2, x_3)^T$$
$$\mathbf{y} = (y_1, y_2, y_3)^T$$

Suppose we want to map 'x' and 'y' to 9-dimensional space. To get the outcome, which would be just scalar, we have to do the calculations shown in the picture below. In this case, the computational complexity will be O(n2).

$$\phi(\mathbf{x}) = (x_1^2, x_1x_2, x_1x_3, x_2x_1, x_2^2, x_2x_3, x_3x_1, x_3x_2, x_3^2)^T$$
$$\phi(\mathbf{y}) = (y_1^2, y_1y_2, y_1y_3, y_2y_1, y_2^2, y_2y_3, y_3y_1, y_3y_2, y_3^2)^T$$

$$\phi(\mathbf{x})^T \phi(\mathbf{y}) = \sum_{i,j=1}^{3} x_i x_j y_i y_j$$

However, by using the "kernel function", which is denoted as 'k(x, y)', instead of doing the complex calculations in the 9-dimensional space, the same outcome can be achieved in the 3-dimensional space by calculating the "dot product" of 'x-transpose' and 'y'. In this case, the computational complexity will be O(n).

$$
\begin{aligned}
k(\mathbf{x}, \mathbf{y}) &= (\mathbf{x}^T \mathbf{y})^2 \\
&= (x_1 y_1 + x_2 y_2 + x_3 y_3)^2 \\
&= \sum_{i,j=1}^{3} x_i x_j y_i y_j
\end{aligned}
$$

In principle, the kernel trick is used to make the transformation of data into higher dimensions much more effective and less costly. The use of the kernel trick is not restricted to the SVM algorithm. The kernel trick can be used with any computations involving the "dot products (x, y)".

Chapter 3: Basics of Data Science Technologies

In the world of technology, Data has described like an "information that a computer is capable of processing and storing". Thanks to our digital lived data has flooded our realities. Our world is drowning with increasing data collected every second, from clicking on a website to monitoring our smartphones and recording our location every second of the day. We could extract alternatives or solutions to our real-world issues that we have not even experienced yet, from the depth of this humongous volume of data. This very process of collecting ideas using mathematical equations and statistics from a measurable set of information can be described as "Data Science". Data scientist's role tends to be very flexible and is often mistaken for the role of a computer scientist or a statistician. Essentially anyone prepared to dig deep into big amounts of data to collect information can be referred to us data science practitioner. For instance, businesses such as "Walmart" keep track and record of customer-made in-store and online purchases providing customized product and service recommendations. Social media platforms such as "Facebook," which enable users to list their "current location", can identify trends of worldwide migration by evaluating the wealth of information that users themselves provide to the platform.

Back in 1960, the earliest recorded use of the word data science was attributed to "Peter Naur", who supposedly used the word "data science" as a replacement for the term computer science and ultimately introduced the word "datalogy". Naur released a book entitled "Concise Survey of Computer Methods" in 1974, with liberal use throughout the book of the term "data science". In 1992, at "The Second Japanese-French Statistics Symposium", the contemporary definition of data science was proposed, with the recognition of the emergence of a new discipline focused primarily on data types, dimensions, and structures.

"Data science continues to evolve as one of the most promising and in-demand career paths for skilled professionals. Today, successful data professionals understand that they must advance past the traditional skills of analyzing large amounts of data, data mining, and programming skills. In order to uncover useful intelligence for their organizations, data scientists must master the full spectrum of the data science life cycle and possess a level of flexibility and understanding to maximize returns at each phase of the process."
– University of California, Berkley

The growing interest of business executives has contributed considerably to the latest increase in the popularity of term data science. A big proportion of journalists and scholarly specialists, however, do not recognize data science as a distinct field of research from the field of statistics. Data science is construed as the popular term for "data mining" and "big data" within the same community. The very definition of the term data science appears to be up for discussion within the tech community. Therefore, largely the field of research a highly versatile skill set including computer programming skills, domain knowledge, proficient statistics abilities and expertise in mathematical algorithms to obtain useful knowledge from large volumes of raw data can be referred to as "data science".

IMPORTANCE AND APPLICATIONS OF DATA SCIENCE

Now that you have a basic understanding of data science, let's look at the significance and applications of data science in our day-to-day lives:

- "Big data and Big Data Analytics" is another 'branch' of data science that organizations use to tackle complicated technological and resource management issues. Later in this book, you will learn more about the concept of big data and big data analytics.

- Data trends have altered dramatically over the last 20 years, indicating a steady rise in unstructured data. It is estimated that "more than 80% of the data we collect will be unstructured by the year 2020". Conventionally, the data we obtained was primarily structured and could easily be analyzed using the simple business intelligence tools, but as shown in the picture below, unstructured and semi-structured data is on the rise. This, in turn, justifies the creation and use of more powerful and sophisticated analytical tools and technologies, than the current business intelligence tools that are unable to process such humungous volume and variety of data. We need more advanced analytical tools and algorithms that can process and analyze unstructured and semi-structured data to provide useful and actionable insights.

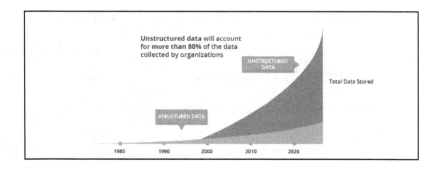

Unstructured data will account for more than 80% of the data collected by organizations

UNSTRUCTURED DATA

Total Data Stored

STRUCTURED DATA

1980   1990   2000   2010   2020

- Companies are always on the verge of understanding their customers' needs better and better. This can now be accomplished by collecting data from current sources such as customer order history, items viewed recently, gender, age and demographics, and using sophisticated analytical tools and algorithms to obtain valuable insights from this data. The use of machine learning algorithms can produce product suggestions for individual clients with greater precision. The "smart" customer is always searching for the most engaging and enhanced user experience, so these analytical tools and algorithms can be used by businesses to gain a competitive advantage and grow their company.

- Data science has made it possible to use sophisticated machine learning algorithms that can be applied across various industrial domains. For instance, developing self-driving vehicles capable of gathering real-time data, using their advanced cameras and sensors to build a map of their environment and make choices about car velocity and other driving maneuvers.

- Data science is used extensively in "predictive analysis". Weather forecasting, for instance, needs data collection and analysis from a multitude of sources including satellites, radars, and aircraft to construct data models that can effectively predict the occurrence of natural disasters such as hurricanes, tornadoes and flash floods.

- The ability of Data science to evaluate the problems facing companies across the industrial spectrum, such as healthcare, travel, finance, retail, and e-commerce, has considerably led to its growing popularity among business leaders.

BIG DATA AND BIG DATA ANALYTICS

In 2001, Gartner defined Big Data as "Data that contains greater variety arriving in increasing volumes and with ever-higher velocity"; which led to the formulation of initial "Three Vs of Big Data". Big data relates to an endlessly flooding avalanche of structured and unstructured data from a multitude of infinite sources of information. These information sets are too big to be analyzed using traditional analytical tools and technologies, but they have a wealth of precious insights hidden in the depth.

The origin of "Big Data" has been traced back to the 1960s and 1970s, when the "Third Industrial Revolution" had just begun to kick in and the growth of relational database had started along with the construction of data centers. But with the high ease of accessibility of free search engines such as "Google" and "Yahoo", free internet entertainment services such as "YouTube" and social media platforms such as "Facebook" and "Twitter", the concept of big data has lately taken center stage. Companies started acknowledging the incredible amount of user data generated through these platforms and services in 2005, and in the same year, the open-source framework called "Hadoop" was developed to collect and analyze these large data dumps available to these companies. A non-relational or distributed database called "NoSQL" began to gain popularity during the same era, because of its capacity to store and extract unstructured data. "Hadoop" enabled businesses to operate with big data at a comparatively low cost and with great ease.

Today, with the rise of cutting-edge technology, not only humans, but we have developed data-generating machines. Smart device technologies such as "Internet of Things" (IoT) and "System Internet" (IoS) have skyrocketed the volume of big data. Our everyday household objects and smart devices are linked to the Internet and are capable of tracking and recording our usage patterns as well as our interactions with these products and directly feeding all this information into big data. The emergence of machine learning technology has further enhanced the daily amount of information produced. It is estimated that "1.7 MB of information per second per person will be produced by 2020". As big data continues to expand, there are still many horizons to be crossed to achieve maximum usability.

"The importance of big data doesn't revolve around how much data you have, but what you do with it. You can take data from any source and analyze it to find answers that enable 1) cost reductions, 2) time reductions, 3) new product development and optimized offerings, and 4) smart decision making."

- SAS

"THE VS OF BIG DATA"

Volume – The "volume" of the given data set must be substantially larger than traditional data sets to be classified as big data. These data sets consist mainly of unstructured data with limited structured and semi-structured data. Input sources such as web pages, search history, mobile apps, and social media platforms can provide data with unknown significance or unstructured data. The company's size and client base is generally proportional to the volume of data the firm can easily obtain.

Velocity – The speed at which data can be collected and the processed refers to the velocity of big data. The combination of on-premise and cloud-based servers is increasingly being used by companies to improve the pace and storage of their data collection. Modern-day "Smart Products and Devices" utilize real-time access to customer information, to provide them with more engaging and improved user experience.

Variety – Conventionally, a data set would comprise of mostly structured data with a small quantity of unstructured and semi-structured data, but the emergence of big data has given rise to new unstructured data types such as video, text, audio that require advanced tools and technologies to clean and process for extraction of meaningful and actionable insights.

Veracity – Veracity is another "V" to be regarded for big data analytics. This relates to the "reliability or quality" of the data. For instance, social media platforms such as "Facebook" and "Twitter" with blogs and posts, flooded with hashtags and acronyms and all types of typing errors can considerably decrease the reliability and accuracy of the data sets.

Value – Data has developed as an inherent currency of its own. Like traditional currencies, big data's ultimate value is directly proportional to the usefulness and quality of insights collected from it.

IMPORTANCE AND APPLICATIONS OF BIG DATA/BIG DATA ANALYTICS

To gain accurate and reliable information from a data set, it is very essential to have a full data set and that can be accomplished with the use of big data technology. The more data we have, the more details and insights can be obtained from it. The future of big data is very promising for obtaining a 360 view of a problem and its underlying solutions. Here are some examples of the application of big data.

Product development – Big data is progressively being used by large and small e-commerce companies to comprehend client requirements and expectations. Companies can create predictive models for launching new products and services using the main features of their past and current products and services and producing a model describing the connection between those features and the business achievement of those products and services. For instance, "Procter & Gamble," a major fast-moving commercial goods company, widely utilizes large information collected from social media websites, test markets, and focus groups to prepare for their new product launch.

Predictive maintenance – A large volume of unstructured data such as error messages, log entries, and ordinary machine temperature must be evaluated along with accessible structured data, such as machine make, model and production year, to avoid potential mechanical and equipment failures. By evaluating this big data set using the necessary analytical instruments, businesses can extend their equipment's shelf life by preparing ahead of time for scheduled maintenance and predicting potential mechanical failures in the future.

Customer experience – The "smart customer" is conscious of all the advances in technology and is only faithful to the most engaging and enhanced user experience available. This has led to a race of the companies to provide distinctive customer experiences analyzing the information collected from customer interactions with the goods and services of the company. Providing personalized recommendations and discount offers, companies can lower the churn rate of their customers and efficiently convert potential leads into paying buyers.

Fraud and compliance – Big data enables identification of data patterns and supports deterrence of possibly fraudulent transactions in the future, by defining data patterns and evaluating historical trends from past fraudulent transactions.

Banks, financial institutions and internet payment services such as "PayPal" are continually tracking and collecting information on customer transactions in an attempt to avoid fraud.

Operational effectiveness – Using predictive analysis of big data, companies can learn and anticipate future demand and product trends by evaluating manufacturing capacity, customer feedback, and information on top-selling items and product returns, to enhance decision-making and generate goods that are in line with current market trends.

Machine learning – For a machine to be able to learn and train on its own it needs a huge quantity of data, i.e. Big Data. A solid training set with structured, semi-structured and unstructured data will help the machine develop a multi-dimensional view of the real world and the problem to be solved.

Drive innovation – By studying and understanding the interactions between individuals and their electronic devices as well as the manufacturers of these devices, companies can create enhanced and innovative goods by examining current product trends and meeting client expectations.

DATA MINING

Data mining technology is defined as "the process of exploring and analyzing large volumes of data to gather meaningful patterns and rules". Data mining comes under the umbrella of data science and is used to construct, artificial intelligence-based machine learning models, for instance, search engine algorithms. Although the procedure of "digging through data" to uncover hidden patterns and predict future events has been around for a while and known as "database knowledge discovery," the term "data mining" was coined as recently as the 1990s.

Data mining consists of three foundational and highly intertwined science disciplines, namely "statistics" (the mathematical study of data relationships), "machine learning algorithms" (algorithms that can be trained with an inherent capability to learn) and "artificial intelligence" (machines that can display human-like intelligence). Data Mining technology has evolved with the introduction of Big data analytics to keep up with the "unlimited potential of big data" and affordable computing power. Using advanced processing speed and power of contemporary computing devices, the once considered tedious, labor-intensive and time-consuming operations have been successfully automated.

"Data mining is the process of finding anomalies, patterns and correlations within large data sets to predict outcomes. Using a broad range of techniques, you can use this information to increase revenues, cut costs, improve customer relationships, reduce risks and more."

– SAS

According to SAS, "unstructured data alone makes up 90% of the digital universe". This big data avalanche does not necessarily ensure more knowledge and understanding. Using data mining technology enables all redundant and unnecessary data noise to be filtered out, so to garner the understanding of applicable information used in the immediate decision-making process.

Importance and applications of Data mining

The applications of data mining techniques are widespread, ranging from retail pricing and promotions to loan risk evaluation by financial organizations and banks. Companies across the industrial spectrum can benefit from the applications of data mining technology. Here are some examples of industrial applications of data mining technology:

Healthcare bio-informatics

Statistical models are used by healthcare practitioners to estimate the probability of patients suffering from one or more health condition considering the risk factors. Genetically transmitted illnesses can be avoided or mediated by modeling the genetic, family and demographic data of the patient from the onset of declining health condition. There is a shortage of healthcare experts in developing countries, so assisted diagnoses and patient prioritization are very critical. Models based on data mining have lately been implemented in these nations to assist with prioritization of patients before healthcare practitioners can achieve and administer therapy in these nations.

Credit Risk Management

Financial organizations and banks implement data mining based tools and models that predict the probability of a prospective credit card customer failing to make their credit payments on time and determining the suitable loan limit that the customer may be eligible for. These data mining models collect and extract information from a multitude of input sources including personal information, customer's financial history, and demographics, among others. The model then offers the interest rate to be obtained from the customer by the organization or bank depending on the assessed risk of lending. For instance, the applicant's credit score is taken into account by data mining models and elevated interest rates are provided to people with low credit score.

Spam filtering

A lot of email clients like "Google mail" and "Yahoo mail" depend on data mining tools to detect and flag email spam and malware. The data mining tools generate insights and understanding that can be used to develop improved safety measures and tools by analyzing hundreds and thousands of shared features of spam and malware. Not only are these applications able to detect spam, but they are also very effective in categorizing spam messages and storing them in a distinct directory, so they never enter the user's inbox.

Marketing

Retail businesses need to know their customer demands and expectations to the dot. Businesses can evaluate customer-related information such as order history, demographics, gender and age by using data mining tools to collect useful customer insights and segment them into organizations based on shared shopping characteristics. Then companies develop distinctive advertising policies and campaigns to target particular groups such as discount offers and product promotions.

Sentiment analysis

Companies can analyze their data from all their social media platforms using a method called "text mining" to know their customer base's "sentiment". This process of understanding emotions of a large group of people towards a specific subject is called "sentiment analysis" and can be performed using data mining tools. Using pattern recognition technology, input data from social media platforms and other associated public content websites are gathered using "text mining" technology and data trends identify that feed into the general knowledge of the subject matter. The "natural language processing" method can be used to further dive into this data to comprehend the human language in a particular context.

Qualitative data mining

The "text mining" method can also be used to conduct qualitative research and obtain insights from large quantities of unstructured data. A recent research study by "University of California, Berkeley" disclosed the use of data mining models in child welfare program studies.

Product recommendation systems

Advance "recommendation systems" are like online retailers' bread and butter. To achieve a competitive edge in the industry, the use of predictive customer behavior analysis is increasing among small and large online businesses. Some of the biggest e-commerce companies, including "Amazon", "Macy's" and "Nordstrom", have invested millions of bucks in developing their proprietary data mining models to forecast market trends and offer their customers more engaging and enhanced user experience. The on-demand entertainment giant "Netflix" purchased an algorithm worth more than a million dollars to improve the precision of their video recommendation system, which allegedly improved the accuracy of the recommendation for "Netflix" by more than 8%.

Artificial Intelligence

Psychology professionals classified "human intelligence" as a powerful combination of a multitude of mental skills including the capacity to learn from life experiences, capacity to adapt to evolving settings, abstract ideas, logical reasoning, perception, language capacity, and problem-solving skills. Not only have human beings experimented with livestock to detect indications of intelligence for the greater purpose, but we have also experimented with devices to impart them as human intelligence. And that's where the "Artificial Intelligence" concept came into being.

The pioneering British computer scientist, Alan Turing, laid the foundation for artificial intelligence technology in the mid-20th century, with the development of an abstract machine with a scanner and limitless memory capable of altering and enhancing his programming that implied a learning capacity. Today, this machine serves as the basis for the development and improvement of the modern computer and is known as "Turing machine." Eventually, in 1956, the term "artificial intelligence" or "AI" was coined and can be defined as the science of the development of machines and computers controlled and operated by human beings, but capable of mirroring and manifesting human intelligence to achieve this.

The ability to learn, reason and perceive are considered as the three fundamental goals of Artificial Intelligence. Some of the core human mental abilities that researchers are aspiring to mimic in computers and machines are:

1. **Knowledge** – The machines require a big amount of information to comprehend and process the world as it is. For the development of artificial knowledge engineering, seamless access to information objects, categories, characteristics and interactions that are stored and managed using data storage is critical.

2. **Learning** – The Evergreen technique of testing and error tends to be the easiest type of teaching for artificial intelligence technology.

3. **Problem Solving** – "The systematic process to reach a predefined goal or solution by searching through a range of possible actions" can be defined as problem-solving.

4. **Reasoning** – The capacity to draw inferences is referred to as the act of reasoning in compliance with the scenario at hand. Two commonly recognized types of reasoning are "deductive reasoning" (assumes the conclusion is true if the assumption is true) and "inductive logic" (even if the assumption is true, the conclusion might or might not be true). One of the most challenging challenges in the growth and promotion of artificial intelligence technology is the implementation of "true reasoning".

5. **Perception** – Perception relates to the process of creating a 3-D view of an object using different sensory organs and is directly influenced by the surrounding environment. Artificial perception has already created self-driving cars and the ability to collect and supply products.

Chapter 4: Machine Learning Library "Scikit-Learn" 101

Machine learning libraries are sensitive routines and functions that are written in any given language. Software developers require a robust set of libraries to perform complex tasks without needing to rewrite multiple lines of code. Machine learning is largely based on mathematical optimization, probability, and statistics.

Python is the language of choice in the field of machine learning credited to consistent development time and flexibility. It is well suited to develop sophisticated models and production engines that can be directly plugged into production systems. One of its greatest assets being an extensive set of libraries that can help researchers who are less equipped with developer knowledge to easily execute machine learning.

"Scikit-Learn" has evolved as the gold standard for machine learning using Python, offering a wide variety of "supervised" and "unsupervised" ML algorithms. It is touted as one of the most user-friendly and cleanest machine learning libraries to date. For example, decision trees, clustering, linear and logistics regressions and K-means. Scikit-learn uses a couple of basic Python libraries: NumPy and SciPy and adds a set of algorithms for data mining tasks including classification, regression, and clustering. It is also capable of implementing tasks like feature selection, transforming data and ensemble methods in only a few lines.

In 2007, David Cournapeau developed the foundational code of "Scikit-Learn" as part of a "Summer of Code" project for "Google". Scikit-learn has become one of Python's most famous open-source machine learning libraries since its launch in 2007. But it wasn't until 2010 that Scikit-Learn was released for public use. Scikit-Learn is an open-sourced and BSD licensed, data mining and data analysis tool used to develop supervise and unsupervised machine learning algorithms build on Python. Scikit-learn offers various ML algorithms such as "classification", "regression", "dimensionality reduction", and "clustering". It also offers modules for feature extraction, data processing, and model evaluation.

Designed as an extension to the "SciPy" library, Scikit-Learn is based on "NumPy" and "matplotlib", the most popular Python libraries. NumPy expands Python to support efficient operations on big arrays and multidimensional matrices. Matplotlib offers visualization tools and science computing modules are provided by SciPy. For scholarly studies, Scikit-Learn is popular because it has a well-documented, easy-to-use and flexible API. Developers can utilize Scikit-Learn for their experiments with various algorithms by only altering a few lines of the code. Scikit-Learn also provides a variety of training datasets, enabling developers to focus on algorithms instead of data collection and cleaning. Many of the algorithms of Scikit-Learn are quick and scalable to all but huge datasets. Scikit-learn is known for its reliability and automated tests are available for much of the library. Scikit-learn is extremely popular with beginners in machine learning to start implementing simple algorithms.

PREREQUISITES FOR APPLICATION OF SCIKIT-LEARN LIBRARY

The Scikit-Learn library is based on the SciPy (Scientific Python), which needs to be installed before using SciKit-Learn. This stack involves the following:

NumPy (Base n-dimensional array package)

"NumPy" is the basic package with Python to perform scientific computations. It includes among other things: "a powerful N-dimensional array object; sophisticated (broadcasting) functions; tools for integrating C/C++ and Fortran code; useful linear algebra, Fourier transform, and random number capabilities". NumPy is widely reckoned as an effective multi-dimensional container of generic data in addition to its apparent scientific uses. It is possible to define arbitrary data types. This enables NumPy to integrate with a broad variety of databases seamlessly and quickly. The primary objective of NumPy is the homogeneity of a multidimensional array. It consists of an element table (generally numbers), all of which are of the same sort and are indicated by tuples of non-negative integers. The dimensions of NumPy are called "axes" and array class is called "ndarray".

Matplotlib (Comprehensive 2D/3D plotting)

"Matplotlib" is a 2-dimensional graphic generation library from Python that produces high-quality numbers across a range of hardcopy formats and interactive environments. The "Python script", the "Python", "IPython shells", the "Jupyter notebook", the web app servers, and select user interface toolkits can be used with matplotlib. Matplotlib attempts to further simplify easy tasks and make difficult tasks feasible. With only a few lines of code, you can produce tracks, histograms, scatter plots, bar graphs, error graphs, etc.

A MATLAB-like interface is provided for easy plotting of the Pyplot Module, especially when coupled with IPython. As a power user, you can regulate the entire line styles, fonts properties, and axis properties, through an object-oriented interface or a collection of features similar to the one provided to MATLAB users.

SciPy (Fundamental library for scientific computing)

SciPy is a "collection of mathematical algorithms and convenience functions built on the NumPy extension of Python", capable of adding more impact to interactive Python sessions, by offering high-level data manipulation and visualization commands and courses for the user. An interactive Python session with SciPy becomes an environment that rivals data processing and system prototyping technologies including "MATLAB, IDL, Octave, R-Lab, and SciLab".

Another advantage of developing "SciPy" on Python, is the accessibility of a strong programming language in the development of advanced programs and specific apps. Scientific apps using SciPy benefit from developers around the globe developing extra modules in countless software landscape niches. Everything produced has been made accessible to the Python programmer, from database subroutines and classes as well as "parallel programming to the web". These powerful tools are provided along with the "SciPy" mathematical libraries.

IPython (Enhanced interactive console)

"IPython (Interactive Python)" is an interface or command shell for interactive computing using a variety of programming languages. "IPython" was initially created exclusively for Python, which supports introspection, rich media, shell syntax, tab completion, and history. Some of the functionalities provided by IPython include: "interactive shells (terminal and Qt-based); browser-based notebook interface with code, text, math, inline plots and other media support; support for interactive data visualization and use of GUI tool kits; flexible interpreters that can be embedded to load into your own projects; tools for parallel computing".

SymPy (Symbolic mathematics)

Developed by Ondřej Čertík and Aaron Meurer, SymPy is "an open-source Python library for symbolic computation". It offers algebra computing abilities to other apps, as a stand-alone app and/or as a library as well as live on the internet applications with "SymPy Live" or "SymPy Gamma". "SymPy" is easy to install and test, because it is completely developed in Python boasting limited dependencies. SymPy involves characteristics ranging from calculus, algebra, discrete mathematics, and quantum physics to fundamental symbolic arithmetic. The outcome of the computations can be formatted as "LaTeX" code. In combination with a straightforward, expandable code base in a widespread programming language, the ease of access provided by SymPy makes it a computer algebra system with comparatively low entry barrier.

Pandas (Data structures and analysis)

Pandas provide highly intuitive and user-friendly high-level data structures. Pandas has achieved popularity in the machine learning algorithm developer community, with built-in techniques for data aggregation, grouping, and filtering as well as results of time series analysis. The Pandas library has two primary structures: one-dimensional "Series" and two-dimensional "Data Frames."

Seaborn (data visualization)

Seaborn is derived from the Matplotlib Library and an extremely popular visualization library. It is a high-level library that can generate specific kind of graph including heat map, time series, and violin plots.

INSTALLING SCIKIT-LEARN

The latest version of Scikit-Learn can be found on "Scikit-Learn.org" and requires "Python (version >= 3.5); NumPy (version >= 1.11.0); SciPy (version >= 0.17.0); joblib (version >= 0.11)". The plotting capabilities or functions of Scikit-learn start with "plot_" and require "Matplotlib (version >= 1.5.1)". Certain Scikit-Learn examples may need additional applications: "Scikit-Image (version >= 0.12.3), Pandas (version >= 0.18.0)".

With the previous installation of "NumPy" and "SciPy", the best method of installing Scikit-Learn is using "pip: pip install -U scikit-learn" or "conda: conda install scikit-learn".

One must make sure that "binary wheels" are utilized when using pip and that "NumPy" and "SciPy" have not been recompiled from source, which may occur with the use of specific OS and hardware settings (for example, "Linux on a Raspberry Pi"). Developing "NumPy" and "SciPy" from source tends to be complicated (particularly on Windows), therefore, they need to be setup carefully making sure optimized execution of linear algebra routines is achievable.

APPLICATION OF MACHINE LEARNING USING SCIKIT-LEARN LIBRARY

To understand how Scikit-Learn library is used in development of machine learning algorithm, let us use the "Sales_Win_Loss data set from IBM's Watson repository" containing data obtained from sales campaign of a wholesale supplier of automotive parts. We will build a machine learning model to predict which sales campaign will be a winner and which will incur a loss.

The data set can be imported using Pandas and explored using Pandas techniques such as "head(), tail() and dtypes()". The plotting techniques from "Seaborn" will be used to visualize the data. To process the data Scikit-Learn's "preprocessing.LabelEncoder()" will be used and "train_test_split()" to divide the data set into a training subset and testing subset.

To generate predictions from our data set, three different algorithms will be used namely, "Linear Support Vector Classification and K-nearest neighbors classifier". To compare the performances of these algorithms Scikit-Learn library technique "accuracy_score" will be used. The performance score of the models can be visualized using Scikit-Learn and "Yellowbrick" visualization.

IMPORTING THE DATA SET

To import the "Sales_Win_Loss data set from IBM's Watson repository", the first step is importing the "Pandas" module using *"import pandas as pd"*.

Then we leverage a variable url as *"https://community.watsonanalytics.com/wp content/uploads/2015/04/WA_Fn-UseC_-Sales-Win-Loss.csv"* to store the URL from which the data set will be downloaded.

Now, *"read_csv() as sales_data = pd.read_csv(url)"* technique will be used to read the above "csv or comma-separated values" file, which is supplied by the Pandas module. The csv file will then be converted into a Pandas data framework, with the return variable as *"sales_data"*, where the framework will be stored.

For new 'Pandas' users, the *"pd.read csv()"* technique in the code mentioned above will generate a tabular data structure called "data framework", where an index for each row is contained in the first column, and the label/name for each column in the first row are the initial column names acquired from the data set. In the above code snippet, the "*sales data*" variable results in a table depicted in the picture below.

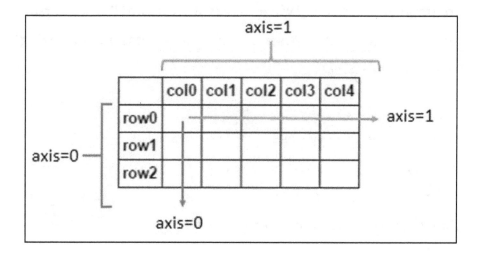

In the diagram above, the "row0, row1, row2" represent individual record index and the "col0, col1, col2" represent the names for individual columns or features of the data set.

With this step, you have successfully stored a copy of the data set and transformed it into a "Pandas" framework!

Now, using the *"head() as Sales_data.head()"* technique the records from the data framework can be displayed as shown below to get a "feel" of the information contained in the data set.

	opportunity number	supplies subgroup	supplies group	region	route to market	elapsed days in sales stage	opportunity result
0	1641984	Exterior Accessories	Car Accessories	Northwest	Fields Sales	76	Won
1	1658010	Exterior Accessories	Car Accessories	Pacific	Reseller	63	Loss
2	1674737	Motorcycle Parts	Performance & Non-auto	Pacific	Reseller	24	Won
3	1675224	Shelters & RV	Performance & Non-auto	Midwest	Reseller	16	Loss

DATA EXPLORATION

Now that we have our copy of the data set which has been transformed it into a "Pandas" data frame, we can quickly explore the data to understand what information can tell can be gathered from it and accordingly to plan a course of action.

In any ML project, data exploration tends to be a very critical phase. Even a fast data set exploration can offer us significant information that could be easily missed otherwise, and this information can propose significant questions that we can then attempt to answer using our project.

Some third-party Python libraries will be used here to assist us with the processing of the data so that we can efficiently use this data with the powerful algorithms of Scikit-Learn. The same *"head()"* technique that we used to see some initial records of the imported data set in the earlier section can be used here. As a matter of fact, *"(head)"* is effectively capable of doing much more than displaying data record and customize the "head()" technique to display only selected records with commands like *"sales_data.head(n=2)"*. This command will selectively display the first 2 records of the data set. At first sight, it's obvious, that columns such as "Supplies Group" and "Region" contain string data, while columns such as "Opportunity Result", "Opportunity Number" etc. are comprised of integer values. It can also be seen that there are unique identifiers for each record in the' Opportunity Number' column.

Similarly, to display select records from the bottom of the table, the *"tail() as sales_data.tail()"* can be used.

To view the different data types available in the data set, the Pandas technique *"dtypes() as sales_data.dtypes"* can be used. With this information, the data columns available in the data framework can be listed with their respective data types. We can figure out, for example, that the column "Supplies Subgroup" is an "object" data type and that the column "Client Size By Revenue" is an "integer data type". So, we have an understanding of columns that either contain integer values or string data.

DATA VISUALIZATION

At this point we are through with basic data exploration steps, so we will not attempt to build some appealing plots to portray the information visually and discover other concealed narratives from our data set.

Of all the available Python libraries providing data visualization features; "Seaborn" is one of the best available options so we will be using the same. Make sure that python plots module provided by "Seaborn" has been installed on your system and ready to be used. Now follow the steps below generate the desired plot for the data set:

Step 1 - Import the "Seaborn" module with the command *"import seaborn as sns"*.

Step 2 - Import the "Matplotlib" module with command *"import matplotlib.pyplot as plt"*.

Step 3 - To set the "background colour" of the plot as white, use command *"sns.set(style="whitegrid", color_codes=True)"*.

Step 4 - To set the "plot size" for all plots, use command *"sns.set(rc={'figure.figsize':(11.7,8.27)})"*.

Step 5 – To generate a "countplot", use command *"sns.countplot('Route To Market',data=sales_data,hue = 'Opportunity Result')"*.

Step 6 – To remove the top and bottom margins, use command *"sns.despine(offset=10, trim=True)"*.

Step 7 – To display the plot, , use command *"plotplt.show()"*.

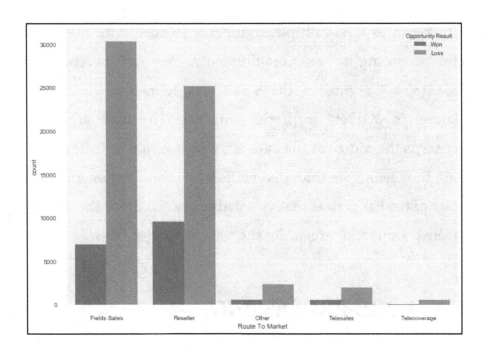

Quick recap - The "Seaborn" and "Matplotlib" modules were imported first. Then the *"set()"* technique was used to define the distinct characteristics for our plot, such as plot style and color. The background of the plot was defined to be white using the code snippet *"sns.set(style= "whitegrid", color codes= True)"*. Then the plot size was define using command *"sns.set(rc={'figure.figsize':(11.7,8.27)})"* that define the size of the plot as "11.7px and 8.27px".

Next the command *"sns.countplot('Route To Market',data= sales data, hue='Opportunity Result')"* was used to generate the plot. The "countplot()" technique enables the creation of a count plot, which can expose multiple arguments to customize the count plot according to our requirements. As part of the first "countplot()" argument, the X-axis was defined as the column "Route To Market" from the data set. The next argument concerns the source of the data set, which would be "sales_data" data framework we imported earlier. The third argument is the color of the bar graphs that was defined as "blue" for the column labeled "won" and "green" for the column labeled "loss".

DATA PRE-PROCESSING

By now you should have a clear understanding of what information is available in the data set. From the data exploration step, we established that majority of the columns in our data set are "string data", but "Scikit-Learn" can only process numerical data. Fortunately, the Scikit-Learn library offers us many ways to convert string data into numerical data, for example, "LabelEncoder()" technique. To transform categorical labels from the data set such as "won" and "loss" into numerical values, we will use the "LabelEncoder()" technique.

Let's look at the pictures below to see what we are attempting to accomplish with the "LabelEncoder()" technique. The first image contains one column labeled "color" with three records namely, "Red", "Green" and "Blue". Using the *"LabelEncoder()"* technique, the record in the same "color" column can be converted to numerical values, as shown in the second image.

	Color
0	Red
1	Green
2	Blue

	Color
0	1
1	2
2	3

Let's begin the real process of conversion now. Using the *"fit transform()"* technique given by *"LabelEncoder()"*, the labels in the categorical column like "Route To Market" can be encoded and converted to numerical labels comparable to those shown in the diagrams above. The function *"fit transform()"* requires input labels identified by the user and consequently returns encoded labels.

To know how the encoding is accomplished, let's go through an example quickly. The code instance below constitutes string data in form of a list of cities such as ["paris", "paris", "tokyo", "amsterdam"] that will be encoded into something comparable to "[2, 2, 1,3]".

Step 1 - To import the required module, use the command *"from sklearn import preprocessing"*.

Step 2 – To create the Label encoder object, use command *"le = preprocessing.LabelEncoder()"*.

Step 3 – To convert the categorical columns into numerical values, use command:

"encoded_value = le.fit_transform(["paris", "paris", "tokyo", "amsterdam"])"

"print(encoded_value) [1 1 2 0]"

And there you have it! We just converted our string data labels into numerical values. The first step was importing the preprocessing module that offers the *"LabelEncoder()"* technique. Followed by development of an object representing the *"LabelEncoder()"* type. Then the *"fit_transform()"* function of the object was used to distinguish between distinct classes of the list ["paris", "paris", "tokyo", "amsterdam"] and output the encoded values of "[1 1 20]".

Did you observe that the *"LabelEncoder()"* technique assigned the numerical values to the classes in alphabetical order according to the initial letter of the classes, for example "(a)msterdam" was assigned code "0", "(p)aris" was assigned code "1" and "(t)okyo" was assigned code "2".

CREATING TRAINING AND TEST SUBSETS

To know the interactions between distinct characteristics and how these characteristics influence the target variable, a ML algorithm must be trained on a collection of information. We need to split the complete data set into two subsets to accomplish this. One subset will serve as the training data set, which will be used to train our algorithm to construct machine learning models. The other subset will serve as the test data set, which will be used to test the accuracy of the predictions generate by the machine learning model.

The first phase in this stage is the separation of feature and target variables using the steps below:

Step 1 – To select data excluding select columns, use command

"select columns other than 'Opportunity Number', 'Opportunity

Result'cols = [col for col in sales_data.columns if col not in ['Opportunity Number','Opportunity Result']]".

Step 2 – To drop these select columns, use command *"dropping the 'Opportunity Number'and 'Opportunity Result' columns*

data = sales_data[cols]".

Step 3 – To assign the Opportunity Result column as "target", use command *"target = sales_data['Opportunity Result']*

data.head(n=2)".

The "Opportunity Number" column was removed since it just acts as a unique identifier for each record. The "Opportunity Result" contains the predictions we want to generate, so it becomes our "target" variable and can be removed from the data set for this phase. The first line of the above code will select all the columns except "Opportunity Number" and "Opportunity Result" in and assign these columns to a variable "cols". Then using the columns in the "cols" variable a new data framework was developed. This is going to be the "feature set". Next, the column "Opportunity Result" from the *"sales_data"* data frame was used to develop a new data framework called "target".

The second phase in this stage concerns the separation of the date frameworks into training and testing subsets using the steps below. Depending on the data set and desired predictions, it needs to be split into training and testing subset accordingly. For this exercise, we will use 75% of the data as a training subset and the rest 25% will be used for the testing subset. We will leverage the *"train_test_split()"* technique in "Scikit-Learn" to separate the data using steps and code as below:

Step 1 – To import the required module, use the command *"from sklearn.model_selection import train_test_split"*.

Step 2 – To separate the data set, use command *"split data set into train and test setsdata_train, data_test, target_train, target_test = train_test_split(data,target, test_size = 0.30, random_state = 10)"*.

With the code above, the *"train_test_split"* module was first imported, followed by the use of *"train_test_split()"* technique to generate "training subset *(data_train, target_train)*" and "testing subset *(data_test, data_train)"*. The *"train_test_split()"* technique's first argument pertains to the features that were divided in the preceding stage, the next argument relates to the target ("Opportunity Result"). The third "test size" argument is the proportion of the data we wish to divide and use as a testing subset. We are using 30% for this example, although it can be any amount. The fourth 'random state' argument is used to make sure that the results can be reproduced every time.

BUILDING THE MACHINE LEARNING MODEL

The "machine_learning_map" provided by Scikit-Learn is widely used to choose the most appropriate ML algorithm for the data set. For this exercise, we will be using "Linear Support Vector Classification" and "K-nearest neighbors classifier" algorithms.

Linear Support Vector Classification

"Linear Support Vector Classification" or "Linear SVC" is a sub-classification of "Support Vector Machine (SVM)" algorithm, which we have reviewed in chapter 2 of this book titled "Machine Learning Algorithms". Using Linear SVC, the data can be divided into different planes so the algorithm can identify the optimal group structure for all the data classes.

Here are the steps and code for this algorithm to build our first ML model:

Step 1 – To import the required modules, use commands *"from sklearn.svm import LinearSVC"* and *"from sklearn.metrics import accuracy_score"*.

Step 2 – To develop an LinearSVC object type, use command *"svc_model = LinearSVC(random_state=0)"*.

Step 3 – To train the algorithm and generate predictions from the testing data, use command *"pred = svc_model.fit(data_train, target_train).predict(data_test)"*.

Step 4 – To display the model accuracy score, use command *"print ('LinearSVC accuracy:', accuracy_score(target_test, pred, normalize = True))"*.

With the code above, the required modules were imported in the first step. We then developed a type of Linear SVC using *"svc_model"* object with "random_state" as '0'. The "random_state" command instructs the built-in random number generator to shuffle the data in a particular order. In step 3, the "Linear SVC" algorithm is trained on the training data set and subsequently used to generate predictions for the target from the testing data. The *"accuracy_score()"* technique was used in the end to verify the "accuracy score" of the model, which could be displayed as "LinearSVC accuracy: 0.777811004785", for instance.

K-nearest Neighbors Classifier

The "k-nearest neighbors(k-NN)" algorithm is referred to as "a non-parametric method used for classification and regression in pattern recognition". In cases of classification and regression, "the input consists of the nearest k closest training examples in the feature space". K-NN is a form of "instance-based learning", or "lazy learning", in which the function is only locally estimated and all calculations are delayed until classification. The output is driven by the fact, whether the classification or regression method is used for k-NN:

- "k-nearest neighbors classification" - The "output" is a member of the class. An "object" is classified by its neighbors' plurality vote, assigning the object to the most prevalent class among its nearest "k-neighbors", where "k" denotes a small positive integer. If k= 1, the "object" is simply allocated to the closest neighbor's class.

- "k-nearest neighbors regression" - The output is the object's property value, which is computed as an average of the k-nearest neighbors values.

A helpful method for both classification and regression can be assigning weights to the neighbors' contributions, to allow closer neighbors to make more contributions in the average, compared to the neighbors located far apart. For instance, a known "weighting scheme" is to assign each neighbor a weight of "$1/d$", where "d" denotes the distance from the neighbor. The neighbors are selected from a set of objects for which the "class" (for "k-NN classification") or the feature value of the "object" (for "k-NN regression") is known.

Here are the steps and code for this algorithm to build our next ML model:

Step 1 – To import required modules, use the command *"from sklearn.neighbors import KNeighborsClassifier"* and *"from sklearn.metrics import accuracy_score"*.

Step 2 – To create object of the classifier, use command *"neigh = KNeighborsClassifier(n_neighbors=3)"*.

Step 3 – To train the algorithm, use command *"neigh.fit(data_train, target_train)"*.

Step 4 – To generate predictions, use command *"pred = neigh.predict(data_test)"*.

Step 5 – To evaluate accuracy, use command *"print ('KNeighbors accuracy score:', accuracy_score(target_test, pred))"*.

With the code above, the required modules were imported in the first step. We then developed the object *"neigh"* of type "KNeighborsClassifier" with the volume of neighbors as *"n_neighbors=3"*. In the next step, the *"fit()"* technique was used to train the algorithm on the training data set. Next, the model was tested on the testing data set using *"predict()"* technique.

Finally, the accuracy score was obtained, which could be "*KNeighbors accuracy score: 0.814550580998*", for instance.

Now that our preferred algorithms have been introduced, the model with the highest accuracy score can be easily selected. But wouldn't it be great if we had a way to compare the distinct models' efficiency visually? In Scikit-Learn, we can use the "Yellowbrick library", which offers techniques for depicting various scoring techniques visually.

Chapter 5: Neural Network Training with TensorFlow

TensorFlow can be defined as a Machine Learning platform providing end-to-end service with a variety of free and open sources. It has a system of multilayered nodes that allow for quick building, training, and deployment of artificial neural networks with large data sets. It is touted as a "simple and flexible architecture to take new ideas from concept to code to state-of-the-art models and publication at a rapid pace". For example, Google uses TensorFlow libraries in their image recognition and speech recognition tools and technologies.

Higher-level APIs such as "tf.estimator" can be used for specifying predefined architectures, such as "linear regressors" or "neural networks". The picture below shows the existing hierarchy of the TensorFlow tool kit:

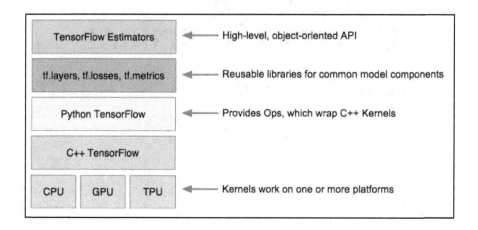

The picture shown below provides the purposes of the different layers:

Toolkit(s)	Description
Estimator (tf.estimator)	High-level, OOP API.
tf.layers/tf.losses/tf.metrics	Libraries for common model components.
TensorFlow	Lower-level APIs

The two fundamental components of TensorFlow are:

1. A "graph protocol buffer"

2. A "runtime" that can execute the graph

The two components mentioned above are similar to the "Python" code and the "Python interpreter". Just as "Python interpreter" can run Python code on several hardware systems, TensorFlow can be operated on various hardware systems, like CPU, GPU, and TPU.

To make a decision regarding which API(s) should be used, you must consider the API offering the highest abstraction level to solve the target problem. Easier to use, but (by design) less flexible, are the greater abstract levels. It is recommended to first begin with the highest-level API and make everything work. If for certain unique modeling issues you need extra flexibility, move one level down. Notice that each level is constructed on the lower-level APIs. It should thus be quite simple to decrease the hierarchy.

For the development of majority of Machine Learning models, we will use "tf.estimator" API, which significantly lowers the number of code lines needed for development. Also, "tf.estimator" is compatible with Scikit-Learn API.

NEURAL NETWORK

The programming of computers needs a human programmer. Many lines of code are used by humans to instruct a computer to provide solutions to our problems. However, the computer can attempt to fix the issue itself through machine learning and neural networks. A neural network is "a function that learns the expected output for a given input from training datasets". For instance, you can train the neural network with many sample bear pictures to construct a neural network that recognizes pictures of a bear. The resulting network operates as functionality to generate the "bear" label as output for the bear picture input. Another more convenient example would be: training the neural network using multiple user activity logs from gaming servers and generate an output stating which users are very likely to convert to paying customer.

Unlike the "Artificial Neural Network" (explained in detail in Chapter 2 of this book), the "Neural Network" features only a single neuron, also called as "perceptron". It is a straightforward and fundamental mechanism which can be implemented with basic math. The primary distinction between traditional programming and a neural network is that computers running on neural network learn from the provided training data set to determine the parameters (weights and prejudice) on their own, without needing any human assistance. Algorithms like "back propagation" and "gradient descent" may be used to train the parameters. It can be stated that the computer tries to increase or decrease every parameter a bit, in the hope that the optimal combination of Parameters can be found, to minimize the error compared with training data set.

FUNDAMENTALS OF NEURAL NETWORK

- Neural networks need clear and informative big data to be trained. You can think of Neural networks as a toddler. They start by observing how their parents are walking. Then they attempt to walk on their own, and the kid learns how to accomplish future tasks with every step. Similarly, the Neural network may fail a few times, but it learns how to generate desired predictions after a few failing attempts.

- For complicated issues such as image processing, it is advisable to use Neural Networks. Neural networks belong to a group of algorithms called "representation learning algorithms". These algorithms are capable of simplifying complicated issues by generating simple (or "representative") form, which tends to be more difficult for conventional (non-representation) algorithms.

- To determine what type of neural network model is suitable for solving the issue at hand, let the data dictate how you fix the issue. For instance, "recurring neural networks" are more appropriate if the issue pertains to sequence generation. While it might be better for you to use "convolutional neural networks" to solve an image-related issue.

- In order to run a deep neural network model, hardware specifications are vital. Neural networks have been around for a long time now, but they are recently experiencing an upsurge primarily credited to the fact that computer resources today are better and more effective. If you want to address a real-life problem using neural network, it is wise to purchase high-end hardware.

TRAINING A NEURAL NETWORK USING TENSORFLOW

In this exercise we will develop a model of neural networks for classifying clothing images such as sneakers and shirts, using TensorFlow library.

I – Import the dataset

For this example, we will be using "Fashion MNIST" data set with 60,000 pictures representing 10 different categories. The low-resolution pictures (28 to 28 pixels) indicate individual clothing items. For the classic MNIST dataset, "Fashion MNIST" is intended as a drop-in replacement. The "MNIST" data set includes pictures of handwritten numbers (0, 1, and so on.) in the same format as the clothing items used in this example. To train the network, we will use 60,000 pictures and 10,000 pictures will be used to assess the accuracy with which the network has learned how to classify pictures.

The "Fashion MNIST" data set is accessible directly from TensorFlow, using the import command as below:

"fashion_mnist = keras.datasets.fashion_mnist (train_images, train_labels), (test_images, test_labels) = fashion_mnist.load_data()"

After the dataset has been loaded system will return 4 different "NumPy arrays" including:

- The *"train_images"* and *"train_labels"* arrays, which serve as the "training dataset" for the model.

- The *"test_images"* and *"test_labels"* arrays, which serve as the "testing dataset" that the model can be tested against.'

Now we need to create labels for an array of integers (0 to 9), corresponding to each category/class of the clothing picture in the data set, using the command below which will look like the table represented in the picture below. This will be useful in generating predictions using our model.

"class_names = ['T-shirt/top', 'Trouser', 'Pullover', 'Dress', 'Coat', 'Sandal', 'Shirt', 'Sneaker', 'Bag', 'Ankle boot']"

Label	Class
0	T-shirt/top
1	Trouser
2	Pullover
3	Dress
4	Coat
5	Sandal
6	Shirt
7	Sneaker
8	Bag
9	Ankle boot

II – Data Exploration

To get some sense of the data set, it can be explored using the commands listed below:

To view the total number of images in the "training data set" and the size of each image – "*train_images.shape*", which will produce the output displayed as "(60000, 28, 28)" stating we have 60,000 pictures of 28 to 28-pixel size.

To view the total number of labels in the "training dataset" – "*len(train_labels)*", which will produce the output displayed as "60000" stating we have 60,000 labels in the training data set.

To view the data type of each label used in the "training dataset"– "*train_labels*", which will produce the output displayed as "*array([9, 0, 0, ..., 3, 0, 5], dtype=uint8)*" stating each label is an integer between o and 9.

To view the total number of images in the "testing dataset" and the size of each image – "*test_images.shape*", which will produce the output displayed as "(10000, 28, 28)" stating we have 10,000 pictures of 28 to 28-pixel size in the testing data set.

To view the total number of labels in the "testing dataset" – "*len(test_labels)*", which will produce the output displayed as "10000" stating we have 10,000 labels in the testing data set.

III – Data Pre-processing

To make the data suitable for training the model, it needs to be pre-processed. It is essential to pre-process the data sets to be used for training and testing in the same manner.

For instance, you notice the first picture in the training data set has the pixel values between 0 and 255, using the commands below:

"plt.figure()"

"plt.imshow(train_images[0])"

"plt.colorbar()"

"plt.grid(False)"

"plt.show()"

These pixel values need to be scaled to fall between 0 to 1, prior to being used as input for the Neural Network model. Therefore, the values need to be divided by 255, for both the data subsets, using commands below:

"train_images = train_images / 255.0"

"test_images = test_images / 255.0"

The final pre-processing step here would be to make sure that the data is is desired format prior to building the Neural Network by viewing the first 20 pictures from the training dataset and displaying the "class name" under each picture, using commands below:

```
"plt.figure(figsize=(10,10))"
"for i in range(20):
  plt.subplot(5,5,i+1)
  plt.xticks([])
  plt.yticks([])
  plt.grid(False)
  plt.imshow(train_images[i], cmap=plt.cm.binary)
  plt.xlabel(class_names[train_labels[i]])"
"plt.show()"
```

IV – Building the Neural Network Model

To build up the "Neural Network", the constituting layers of the model first need to be configured and only then the model can be compiled.

Configuring the layers

The "layers" are the fundamental construction block of a neural network. These "layers" take out information from the data entered generating representations that tend to be extremely valuable addressing the problem.

Majority of "deep learning" involves stacking and linking fundamental layers together. The parameters that are learned during practice are available in most of the layers, like "tf.keras.layers.Dense". To configure the required layers, use command below:

"model = keras.Sequential([

keras.layers.Flatten(input_shape=(28, 28)),

keras.layers.Dense(128, activation=tf.nn.relu),

keras.layers.Dense(10, activation=tf.nn.softmax)

])"

The *"tf.keras.layers.Flatten"* is the first layer in this network, which turns the picture format from a 2-dimesnional array of 28x28 size to a 1-dimension array with "28x28 = 784" pixels. Consider this layer as unchained rows of pixels in the picture that arranged these pictures but without any learning parameters and capable of only altering the data.

The network comprises of a couple of *"tf.keras.layers.Dense"* layers after pixels are flattened. These are neural layers that are fully or densely connected. There are 128 nodes or neurons in the first Dense layer. The succeeding and final layer is a 10-node layer of *"Softmax"*, which generated an array of ten different probability scores amounting to "1". Every single node includes a probability score indicating that one of the ten classes is likely to contain the existing picture.

Compiling the model

Before being able to train the model, some final tweaks are needed to be made in the model compilation step, such as:

Loss function— This provides a measure of the model's accuracy during training. This feature should be minimized so that the model is "directed" in the correct direction.

Optimizer —These are the updates made to the model based on the data it can view as well as its "loss function".

Metrics — Used for monitoring the training and testing procedures. For example, the code below utilizes accuracy, measured by computing the fraction of the pictures that were classified accurately.

"model.compile(optimizer='adam',

  loss='sparse_categorical_crossentropy',

  metrics=['accuracy'])"

V – Training the Model

The steps listed below are used to train the "Neural Network Model":

- Feed the training data to the model, using *"train_images"* and *"train_labels"* arrays.

- Allow the network to learn an association of pictures and corresponding labels.

- Generate predictions using the model for a predefined test data set, for example, the *"test_images"* array. Then the predictions must be verified by matching the labels from the *"test_labels"* array.

You can begin to train the network, by utilizing the *"model.fit"* method. To verify the system is a "fit" for the training data, use command *"model.fit(train_images, train_labels, epochs=5)"*.

The epochs are displayed as below, suggesting that the model has reached accuracy of around 0.89 or 89% of the training data:

"Epoch 1/5

60000/60000 [==============================] - 4s 75us/sample - loss: 0.5018 - acc: 0.8241

Epoch 2/5

60000/60000 [==============================] - 4s 71us/sample - loss: 0.3763 - acc: 0.8643

Epoch 3/5

60000/60000 [==============================] - 4s 71us/sample - loss: 0.3382 - acc: 0.8777

Epoch 4/5

60000/60000   [===============================]   -   4s
72us/sample - loss: 0.3138 - acc: 0.8846

Epoch 5/5

60000/60000   [===============================]   -   4s
72us/sample - loss: 0.2967 - acc: 0.8897

<tensorflow.python.keras.callbacks.History at 0x7f65fb64b5c0>"

VI – Measuring the accuracy of the Neural Network Model

To test the accuracy of the network, it must be verified against the testing data set using commands below:

"test_loss, test_acc = model.evaluate(test_images,
test_labels)"
"print('Test accuracy:', test_acc)"

The output can be obtained as shown below, which suggests that the accuracy of the test result is around 0.86 or 86%, which is slightly less that the accuracy of the training data set. This is a classic example of "overfitting", when the performance or accuracy of the model is lower on new input or testing data than the training data.

"10000/10000 [==============================] - 1s 51us/sample - loss: 0.3653 - acc: 0.8671

Test accuracy: 0.8671"

VII – Generate predictions using the Neural Network Model

Now that our model has been trained sufficiently, we are ready to generate predictions from the model, using command "predictions = model.predict(test_images)".

In the code below, the network has generated a prediction for labels of each picture in the testing data set. The prediction is generated as an array of ten integers with the "confidence" index for each of the ten categories (in referring to the import data stage) corresponding to the test picture.

"predictions[0]"

"array([6.58371528e-06, 1.36480646e-10, 4.17183337e-08, 1.15178166e-10,

8.30939484e-07, 1.49914682e-01, 3.11488043e-06, 4.63472381e-02,

6.10820061e-05, 8.03666413e-01], dtype=float32)"

To view the label with the highest "confidence" index, using command "np.argmax (predictions[0])".

A result "9", will suggest that the model has maximum confidence on the test image belonging to "class_names[9]" or according to our labels table, ankle boot. To verify this prediction, use command "test_labels[0]", which should generate output as "9".

To view the whole set of predictions for the ten classes, use command below:

```
"def plot_image(i, predictions_array, true_label, img):
  predictions_array, true_label, img =
predictions_array[i], true_label[i], img[i]
  plt.grid(False)
  plt.xticks([])
  plt.yticks([])

  plt.imshow(img, cmap=plt.cm.binary)

  predicted_label = np.argmax(predictions_array)
  if predicted_label == true_label:
    color = 'blue'
  else:
    color = 'red'

  plt.xlabel('{} {:2.0f}%
({})'.format(class_names[predicted_label],
                100*np.max(predictions_array),
                class_names[true_label]),
                color=color)

def plot_value_array(i, predictions_array, true_label):
  predictions_array, true_label = predictions_array[i],
```

true_label[i]
 plt.grid(False)
 plt.xticks([])
 plt.yticks([])
 thisplot = plt.bar(range(10), predictions_array,
color='#777777')
 plt.ylim([0, 1])
 predicted_label = np.argmax(predictions_array)

 thisplot[predicted_label].set_color('red')
 thisplot[true_label].set_color('blue')"

Now, for example, you may want to generate a prediction for a specific picture in the testing data set. You can do this using the command below:

"Grab an image from the test dataset
img = test_images[0]
print(img.shape)"

"(28, 28)"

To use the "tf.keras" models to generate this prediction, the picture must be added to a list, since these models have been optimized to generate predictions on a "collection of dataset" at a time. Use the command below to accomplish this:

*"# Add the image to a batch where it's the only member.
img = (np.expand_dims(img,0))*

print(img.shape)"

"(1, 28, 28)"

Now, to generate the prediction for the picture using "tf.keras" use the command below:

*"predictions_single = model.predict(img)
print(predictions_single)"*

The predictions generated will resemble the code below:

*"[[6.5837266e-06 1.3648087e-10 4.1718483e-08
1.1517859e-10 8.3093937e-07*

*1.4991476e-01 3.1148918e-06 4.6347316e-02
6.1082108e-05 8.0366623e-01]]"*

To generate a graph or plot for the prediction (as shown in the picture below), use command below:

"plot_value_array(0, predictions_single, test_labels)
plt.xticks(range(10), class_names, rotation=45)
plt.show()"

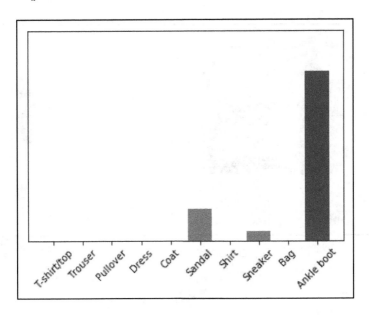

The "model.predict" generated the output as a "list of lists", for every single picture in the testing data set. To generate predictions specifically for the specific image we used earlier, use command below:

"prediction_result = np.argmax(predictions_single[0])
print(prediction_result)"

The output or prediction generated should be "9" as we obtained earlier.

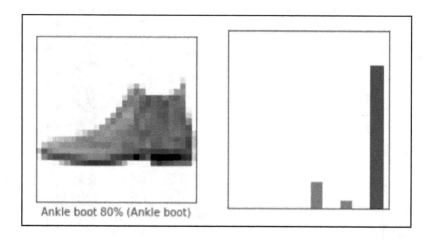

Ankle boot 80% (Ankle boot)

CHAPTER 6: DATA PRE-PROCESSING AND CREATION OF TRAINING DATA SET

Data Preprocessing is a "data mining technique, which is used to transform raw data into a comprehensible and effective format". Real-world data tend to lack certain behaviors or trends and is almost always incomplete, inconsistent and/or missing attribute values, flooded with errors or outliers. Preprocessing data is a proven way to solve such problems. This raw data or real data from the world can not be readily transmitted through a machine learning model. Therefore, before feeding real-world data to a machine learning model, we need to clean and pre-process it.

OVERVIEW DATA PREPROCESSING

Data Cleaning

Many meaningless and missing sections can be found in the data. "Data cleaning" is performed to manage these inadequacies and constitutes handling data set that is missing values and consists of noisy data.

Missing Data

In this scenario, certain significant information in the data set is missing. It can be dealt with in different respects such as:

Ignoring the tuples: This strategy is appropriate only if the dataset is big and numerous values within a tuple are lacking.

Fill the missing values: This assignment can be done in different ways such as: manually completing the missing values using the mean attribute or the most relevant value.

Noisy Data

"Noisy data" is useless data that machines or the machine learning model is unable to interpret. It can be generated as a result of defective data collection or mistakes in data entry, among others. It can be addressed using the methods below:

Binning Method: This technique operates on sorted data to smoothen it out. The entire data set is split into equivalent size sections and then different techniques are used to finish the job. Each section is fixed individually. To fix the entire data set in ago, all data points in a section can be substituted with its "mean" or most probable values.

Regression: In this case, data can be smoothed out by fitting into a "regression function", which can be either "linear" (with one autonomous variable) or "multiple" (with various autonomous variables).

Clustering: This technique is used to group comparable data points into a cluster. The outliers could be obtained with data points falling outside of the clusters or could not be detected.

Data Transformation

This technique is used to convert the data into a format which is suitable for the data mining method. This includes the following ways:

Normalization: This technique is used to scale data values within a defined range, for example, "-1.0 to 1.0" or "0.0 to 1.0".

Attribute Selection: New data attributes can be generated from an existing data set of characteristics, using this technique to assist in the data mining process.

Discretization: This technique is used to "replace raw values of numerical attributes with interval or conceptual levels".

Generation of the concept of hierarchy: This technique is used to transform lower-level data attributes to higher level in the hierarchical setup. For example, you can convert the attribute "city" to "country."

Data Reduction

"Data mining" is a method used for analysis and extraction of insights from Big data. In such instances, analysis becomes more and more difficult to work with given the enormity of data. We use data reduction method to reduce the volume of data set to an optimal and manageable volume. With this method, the cost of data storage and analysis can be significantly lowered while improving the effectiveness of the data storage. It can be dealt with in different respects such as:

Data Cube Aggregation: This technique is used to apply "aggregation operation" to data to effectively build data cubes.

Selection of attribute subset: This technique is used to ensure that only necessary data attributes are used and the not so relevant attributes can be discarded. To perform attribute selection, the "level of significance" and "p-value of the attribute" can be leveraged. The attribute with "p-value" higher than the "significance level" can be removed to obtain the optimal volume of the data set.

Numerosity Reduction: This technique allows the data model to be stored instead of the whole data set or raw data collected from various input sources, for instance, "Regression Models".

Dimensionality Reduction: This technique uses encoding mechanisms to reduce the volume of the data set. If initial data set can be recovered after reconstruction from compressed data set, this reduction in dimensions of the data set is known as "lossless reduction", otherwise it is referred to as "loss reduction". The two efficient techniques of reducing data set "dimensionality" are: "Wavelet transforms" and "PCA (Principal Component Analysis)".

STEPS OF DATA PRE-PROCESSING

I – Import the data library

There is a wide variety of data libraries available that you can choose to meet your data requirements, such as:

"Pandas": Widely used for data visualization and data manipulation processes.

"NumPy": A basic package to perform scientific computations using Python.

"Matplotlib": A standard Python Library used by data scientists to create 2-D plots and graphs.

"Seaborn": Seaborn is derived from the "Matplotlib" library and an extremely popular visualization library.

For example, you can use the main libraries from "Pandas", "NumPy" and "time"; data visualization libraries from "Matplotlib" and "Seaborn"; and Scikit-Learn libraries for the data preprocessing techniques and algorithms.

To import the libraries mentioned above, use the code below:

For main libraries

"import pandas as pd

import numpy as np

import time"

For visualization libraries

"from matplotlib import pyplot as plt
import seaborn as sns
from mpl_toolkits.mplot3d import Axes3D
plt.style.use('ggplot')"

For Scikit-Learn libraries

"from sklearn.neighbors import KNeighborsClassifier
from sklearn.model_selection import train_test_split
from sklearn.preprocessing import normalize
from sklearn.metrics import
*confusion_matrix,accuracy_score,precision_score,recall_*
score,f1_score,matthews_corrcoef,classification_report,r
oc_curve
from sklearn.externals import joblib
from sklearn.preprocessing import StandardScaler
from sklearn.decomposition import PCA"

II – Data exploration

To get some sense of the imported dataset in Pandas, use the code below:

"# Read the data in the CSV file using pandas
df = pd.read_csv('../input/creditcard.csv')
df.head()"

III – Check for missing values

It is essential to comprehend the concept of missing values to be able to effectively manage data. If the researcher does not handle the missing values correctly, they may end up drawing incorrect data inferences. Because of improper handling, the results produced will be different from those with missing values. You can apply any of the techniques below to deal with missing data values in your data set:

1.   Ignore the data row

This is generally performed when the "class label" is missing or if a multiple data attribute is missing in the row, assuming the data mining objective is classification. However, if the proportion of such rows with missing class labels is high, you will get bad output.

For instance, database with enrolment data for the student (age, SAT score, address, etc.) containing a column with "Low", "Medium" and "High" to classify their achievement in college. Assuming the objective is to construct a model that predicts the college achievement of a student. Data rows that do not include the achievement column are not helpful to generate predictions regarding the success of the student, so they can be overlooked and deleted before the algorithm is executed.

2. Use a global constant to fill in for missing values

In this technique, an appropriate and new global constant value is selected, such as "unknown," "N / A" or "minus infinity", which is then used to fill all the missing values. This technique is employed when the concerted effort to predict the missing value just doesn't make sense. Let's consider the student enrollment database example again, assume that some students lack information on the 'state of residence' attribute. It doesn't make sense to fill it with some random state instead of using "N/A".

3. Use attribute mean

This technique is used to replace an attribute's missing values with the "mean or median value (if it's discrete)", for a specific attribute in the database. For instance, in a US family income database, if the average income of a family is X, that value can be used to replace missing values in the other family records.

4.   Using attribute mean for all samples belonging to the same class

This technique is used to restrict the calculations to a particular class in order to obtain a value that is applicable to the row that we are searching for in lies of using the "mean (or medians)" of a particular attribute calculated by searching all the rows of the database. For example, if you have an automobile price database that classifies vehicles, among other things, into "Luxury" and "Low Budget". It is likely more precise to replace the missing price of a "luxury car" with the average price of all luxury vehicles instead of the value obtained after factoring in "low budget cars".

5.   Use data mining algorithm to predict the most probable value

Data mining algorithms such as "Regression", "inference-based tools using Bayesian formalism", "decision trees", "clustering algorithms (K-Mean\Median, etc.)" can be used to determine the probable value of the data attribute. For instance, "clustering algorithms" could be employed to produce a cluster of rows that are then used to calculate the mean or median of the attribute as indicated earlier in Technique 3. Another instance might be to use a "decision tree" to generate a prediction for the most probable value of the missing attribute by taking into account all other attributes in the data set.

IV – Dealing with Categorical Data values

Categorical attributes can only take on a restricted amount of feasible values, which are generally fixed. For instance, if a dataset is about user-related data, then characteristics such as 'nation', 'gender', 'age group', etc. will constitute the data set. Alternatively, you will find attributes such as 'product type', 'manufacturer', 'vendor', and so on if your data set pertains to a commodity or product.

In the context of the data set, these are all categorical attributes. Typically, these attributes are stored as text values representing different characteristics of the observations. Gender is defined, for instance, as "male" or "female", and product type could be defined as "electronics", "apparel", "food" and so on.

There are three types of categorical data:

- **Nominal** – The types of attributes where categories are only labeled and have no order of succession are called "nominal features". For example, gender could be 'male' (M) or 'female' (F) and have no order of precedence.

- **Ordinal** – The types of attributes where categories are labeled with an order of precedence are called "ordinal features". For example, an economic status feature can contain three categories: "low", "medium" and "high", which have an inherent order associated with them.

- **Continuous** – The types of attributes where categories are numerical variables with infinite values ranging between two defined values are called "continuous features".

CHALLENGES OF CATEGORICAL DATA

- Categorical attributes can contain multiple levels, called "high cardinality" (e.g. states, towns or URLs), where most levels appear in a relatively smaller number of instances.

- Various ML models are algebraic, such as "regression" and "SVM", which require numerical input. Categories have to be changed first to numbers to use these models before the machine learning algorithm can be applied.

- While some machine learning packages or libraries are capable of automatically transforming the categorical data into numeric, depending on the default embedded technique, a variety of machine learning libraries don't support categorical data inputs.

- Categorical data for the computer does not translate the context or background, that people can readily associate with and comprehend. For instance, consider a function called "City" with different city names like "New York", "New Jersey", and "New Delhi". People know that "New York" is strongly linked to "New Jersey" being two neighboring states of America, while "New York" and "New Delhi" are very distinct. On the other hand, for the machine, all three cities just denote three distinct levels of the same "City" function. Without specifying adequate context through data for the model, differentiating between extremely distinct levels will be difficult for it.

ENCODING CATEGORICAL DATA

Machine learning models are built on mathematical equations, so it is easy to comprehend that maintaining the categorical data in equations would cause issues since equations are primarily driven by numbers alone. To cross this hurdle, the categorical features can be encoded to numeric quantities.

The encoding techniques below will be described using example of an "airline carrier" column from a make-believe airline database, for ease of understanding. However, it is possible to extend the same techniques to any desired column.

1. Replacing the categorical values

This is a fundamental technique of replacing the categorical data values with required integers. The *"replace()"* function in Pandas, can be used for this technique. Depending on your business requirements, desired numbers can be easily assigned to the categorical values.

2.   Encoding Labels

The technique of converting categorical values in a column to a number is called as "label encoding". Numerical labels always range from "0" to "n categories-1". Encoding a group of categories to a certain numerical value and then encoding all other categories to another numerical value can be done using the *"where()"* function in NumPy. For example, one could encode all the "US airline carriers" to value "1" and all other carriers can be given value "0". You can perform similar label encoding using "Scikit-Learn's LabelEncoder".

Label encoding is fairly intuitive and simple and produces satisfactory performance from your learning algorithm. However, the algorithm is at a disadvantage and may misinterpret numerical values. For example, an algorithm may confuse whether the "U.S. airline carrier" (encoded to 6) should be given 6 times more weight "U.S. airline carrier" (encoded to 1).

3.   One-Hot encoding

To resolve the misinterpretation issue of the machine learning algorithm generated by the "label encoding" technique, each categorical data value can be transformed into a new column and that new column can be allocated a '1' or '0' (True/False) value, and is called as "one-hot encoding".

Of all the machine learning libraries in the market that offer "one-hot encoding", the easiest one is *"get_dummies()"* technique in "Pandas", which is appropriately titled given the fact that dummy/indicator data variables such as "1" or "0" are created. In its preprocessing module, Scikit-Learn also supports "one-hot encoding" in its pre-processing module via "LabelBinarizer" and "OneHotEncoder" techniques.

While "one-hot encoding" addresses the issue of misinterpreted category weights, it gives rise to another issue. Creation of multiple new columns to solve this category weight problem for numerous categories can lead to a "curse of dimensionality". The logic behind "curse of dimensionality" is that some equations simply stop functioning correctly in high-dimensional spaces.

4.   Binary encoding

This method initially encodes the categories as "ordinal", then converts these integers into a binary string, and then divides digits of that binary code into distinct columns. Therefore, the data is encoded in only a few dimensions, unlike the "one-hot encoding" method.

There are several options to implement binary encoding in your machine learning model but the easiest option is to install "category_encoders" library. This can be done using "pip install category_encoders" on cmd.

5. Backward difference encoding

This "backward difference encoding" method falls within the "contrast coding scheme" for categorical attributes. A "K" category or level characteristic typically enters a "regression" as a series of dummy "K-1" variables. This technique works by drawing a comparison between the "mean" of the dependent variable for a level with the "mean" of the dependent variable in the preceding stage. This kind of encoding is widely used for a "nominal" or an "ordinal "variable".

The code structure for this technique is quite similar to any other technique in the "category_encoders" library, except the

run   command   for   this   technique   is
"BackwardDifferenceEncoder".

6.   Miscellaneous features

You may sometimes deal with categorical columns that indicate
the range of values in observation points, for instance, an 'age'
column can contain categories such as '0-20', '20-40', '40-60' etc.
While there may be many methods to handle such attributes, the
most popular ones are:

A. Dividing the categorical value ranges into two distinct
   columns, by first creating a dummy data frame with just
   one feature as "age" and then splitting the column on the
   delimiter "(-)" into two columns "start" and "end" using
   "split()" and "lambda()" functions .

B. Replacing the categorical value ranges with a selected
   measure like the mean value of the range, using the
   function "split_mean()".

V – Splitting the data set into Training and Testing data subsets

The machine learning algorithms are required to learn from sample data set to be able to generate predictions from the input data set. In general, we divide the data set into a proportion of 70:30 or 80:20, which means that 70% of the data is used as the training subset and 30% of the data is used as the testing subset. However, this split ratio is adjusted according to the form and size of the data set.

It is almost impossible and futile to manually split the data set while making sure the data set is divided randomly. The Scikit-Learn library offers us a tool called the "Model Selection library", to assist with this task. There is a "class" in the Scikit-Learn library called *"train_test_split"*. Using this, we can readily divide the data set into the "training" and "testing" datasets in desired ratios. Some parameters to consider while using this tool are:

- **Test_size** - It helps in determining the size of the data to be divided as the testing data set, like a fraction of the total data set. For example, entering 0.3 as the "test_size" value, the data set will be divided at 30 percent as the test data set. If you specify this parameter, the next parameter may be ignored.

- **Train_size** – This parameter is only specified if the "test_size" has not been specified already. The process works similar to the "test_size" function, except that the percentage of the data set specified is for the "training set".

- **Random_state** - An integer is entered here for the Scikit-Learn class, based on which the "random number generator" will be activated during the data set split. Alternatively, an instance of "RandomState" class can b entered that will then generate random numbers. If you don't enter either of the functions, the default will be activated which leverages the "RandomState" instance used by "np.random".

For example, the data set in the picture below can be split into two subsets: 'X' subset for the "independent features" and 'Y' subset for the "dependent variables" and also happens to be the last column of the data set.

Country	Age	Salary	Purchased
France	44	72000	No
Spain	27	48000	Yes
Germany	30	54000	No
Spain	38	61000	No
Germany	40	nan	Yes
France	35	58000	Yes
Spain	nan	52000	No
France	48	79000	Yes
Germany	50	83000	No
France	37	67000	Yes

Now we can use the code below to split the "x" data set into two subsets: "xTrain" and "xTest" and likewise, split the "y" data set into two subsets "yTrain" and "yTest".

"from sklearn.model_selection import train_test_split

xTrain, xTest, yTrain, yTest = train_test_split(x, y,

test_size = 0.2, random_state = 0)"

According to the code above, the test data set size will be 0.2 or 20% of the entire data set and the remaining 80% of the data set will be used for the training data set.

PYTHON TIPS AND TRICKS FOR DEVELOPERS

Python was first implemented in 1989 and is regarded as highly user-friendly and simple to learn programming language for entry-level coders and amateurs. This is ideal for individuals newly interested in programming or coding and requires to comprehend programming fundamentals. This stems from the fact that Python reads almost the same as the English language. Therefore, it requires less time to understand how the language works and focus can be directed in learning the basics of programming.

Python is an interpreted language that supports automatic memory management and object-oriented programming. This extremely intuitive and flexible programming language can be used for coding projects such as machine learning algorithms, web applications, data mining and visualization, game development.

Some of the tips and tricks you can leverage to sharpen up your Python programming skill set are:

In-place swapping of two numbers:

"x, y = 100, 200

print(x, y)

x, y = y, x

print(x, y)"

Resulting Output =

100 200

200 100

Reversing a string:

"a ="machine""

"print("Reverse is", a[::-1])"

Resulting Output =

Reverse is enihcam.

Creating a single string from multiple list elements:

"a = ["machine", "learning", "algorithms"]"

print(" ".join(a))"

Resulting Output =

machine learning algorithms

Stacking of comparison operators:

"n = 10

result = 1 < n < 20

print(result)

result = 1 > n <= 9

print(result)"

Resulting Output =

True

False

Print the file path of the imported modules:

"import os;

import socket;

print(os)

print(socket"

Resulting Output =

"<module 'os' from '/usr/lib/python3.5/os.py'>

<module 'socket' from '/usr/lib/python3.5/socket.py'>"

Use of enums in Python:

"*class MyName:*

  Geeks, For, Geeks = range(3)

print(MyName.Geeks)

print(MyName.For)

print(MyName.Geeks)"

Resulting Output =

2

1

2

Return multiple values from functions:

"def x():

   return 1, 2, 3, 4

a, b, c, d = x()

print(a, b, c, d)"

Resulting Output =

"1 2 3 4"

Identify the value with highest frequency:

"test = [1, 2, 3, 4, 2, 2, 3, 1, 4, 4, 4]

print(max(set(test), key = test.count))"

Resulting Output =

4

Check the memory usage of an object:

"import sys

x = 1

print(sys.getsizeof(x))"

Resulting Output =

28

Printing a string N times:

"n = 2;

a ="machinelearning";

*print(a * n);"*

Resulting Output =

machinelearningmachinelearningmachinelearning

Identify anagrams:

```
"from collections import Counter
def is_anagram(str1, str2):
    return Counter(str1) == Counter(str2)
print(is_anagram('geek', 'eegk'))


print(is_anagram('geek', 'peek'))"
```

Resulting Output =

True

False

Transposing a matrix:

```
"mat = [[1, 2, 3], [4, 5, 6]]
zip(*mat)"
```

Resulting Output =

[(1, 4), (2, 5), (3, 6)]

Print a repeated string without using loops:

"print "machine"*3+' '+"learning"*4"

Resulting Output =

Machinemachinemachine learninglearninglearninglearning

Measure the code execution time:

"import time"

"startTime = time.time()"

" write your code or functions calls"

" write your code or functions calls"

"endTime = time.time()"

"totalTime = endTime – startTime"

"print('Total time required to execute code is=' , totalTime)"

Resulting Output =

Total time

Obtain the difference between two lists:

"list1 = ['Scott', 'Eric', 'Kelly', 'Emma', 'Smith']

list2 = ['Scott', 'Eric', 'Kelly']

set1 = set(list1)

set2 = set(list2)

list3 = list(set1.symmetric_difference(set2))

print(list3)"

Resulting Output =

list3 = ['Emma', 'Smith]

Calculate the memory being used by an object in Python:

"import sys"

"list1 = ['Scott', 'Eric', 'Kelly', 'Emma', 'Smith']"

"print("size of list = ",sys.getsizeof(list1))"

"name = 'pynative.com'"

"print('size of name =' ,sys.getsizeof(name))"

Resulting Output =

('size of list = ', 112)

('size of name = ', 49)

Removing duplicate items from the list:

"listNumbers = [20, 22, 24, 26, 28, 28, 20, 30, 24]"

"print ('Original=' , listNumbers)"

"listNumbers = list(set(listNumbers))"

"print ('After removing duplicate= ' , listNumbers)"

Resulting Output =

"'Original= ', [20, 22, 24, 26, 28, 28, 20, 30, 24]"

"'After removing duplicate= ', [20, 22, 24, 26, 28, 30]"

Find if a list contains identical elements:

"*listOne = [20, 20, 20, 20]*

print('All element are duplicate in listOne',
listOne.count(listOne[0]) == len(listOne))

listTwo = [20, 20, 20, 50]

print('All element are duplicate in listTwo',
listTwo.count(listTwo[0]) == len(listTwo))"

Resulting Output =

"'All element are duplicate in listOne', True"

"'All element are duplicate in listTwo', False"

Efficiently compare two unordered lists:

"from collections import Counter

one = [33, 22, 11, 44, 55]

two = [22, 11, 44, 55, 33]

print('is two list are b equal', Counter(one) ==
Counter(two))"

Resulting Output =

"'is two list are b equal', True"

Check if list contains all unique elements:

"def isUnique(item):

tempSet = set()

return not any(i in tempSet or tempSet.add(i) for i in item)

listOne = [123, 345, 456, 23, 567]

print('All List elements are Unique' , isUnique(listOne))

listTwo = [123, 345, 567, 23, 567]

print('All List elements are Unique' , isUnique(listTwo))"

Resulting Output =

"All List elements are Unique True"

"All List elements are Unique False"

Convert Byte into String:

"byteVar = b"pynative""

"str = str(byteVar.decode('utf-8'))"

"print('Byte to string is' , str)"

Resulting Output =

"Byte to string is pynative"

Merge two dictionaries into a single expression:

"currentEmployee = {1: 'Scott', 2: 'Eric', 3:'Kelly'}

formerEmployee = {2: 'Eric', 4: 'Emma'}

def merge_dicts(dictOne, dictTwo):

dictThree = dictOne.copy()

dictThree.update(dictTwo)

return dictThree

print(merge_dicts(currentEmployee, formerEmployee))"

CONCLUSION

Thank you for making it through to the end of *Python Machine Learning: Discover the essentials of machine learning, data analysis, data science, data mining and artificial intelligence using Python Code with Python tricks*, let's hope it was informative and able to provide you with all of the tools you need to achieve your goals whatever they may be.

The next step is to make the best use of your new-found wisdom in today's cutting-edge technologies, primarily machine learning, that have created the "Silicon Valley" powerhouse. Today, machine learning technology has given rise to sophisticated machines, which can study human behavior and activity in order to recognize fundamental patterns of human behavior and exactly predict which products and services consumer may be interested in. Under the side of their business model, businesses with an eye for the future gradually become technology firms with systems built upon machine learning algorithms. Consider some of the most innovative tech gadgets of this era such as "Amazon Alexa", "Apple's Siri" and "Google Home", what they all have in common is their underlying machine learning capabilities. Now that you have finished reading this book and mastered the use of Scikit-Learn and TensorFlow libraries, you are all set to start developing your own Python machine learning model using all the open sources readily available and explicitly mentioned in this book for that purpose.

If you found this useful you could also like:

MACHINE LEARNING *PROGRAMMING*

This Book Includes: Machine Learning for Beginners + Machine Learning Mathematics. An Introduction Guide to Understand Data Science Through the Business Application

By Samuel Hack

I would like to thank you for reading this book and if you enjoyed it I would appreciate your review on Amazon!

CPSIA information can be obtained
at www.ICGtesting.com
Printed in the USA
LVHW011307221220
674886LV00001B/102

9 781801 142946